"He's got my leg!"

"I knew what it was as soon as it grabbed me. You always think it's something in the movies. You don't think it's going to happen to you."

"Help me please, a fish is killing me."

"He took two chomps and that was it. I felt his rough skin with my hands . . ."

"Help me, for God's sake help me."

"Let me die."

. . . TERRIFYING TRUE WORDS FROM REAL VICTIMS OF SHARK ATTACKS!

SHARK ATTACKS

Alex MacCormick

St. Martin's Paperbacks

Published by arrangement with Constable and Company Ltd.

SHARK ATTACKS

ISBN: 0-312-96618-0

Printed in the United States of America

Constable and Company Ltd. edition published 1996
St. Martin's Paperbacks edition / July 1998

St. Martin's Paperbacks are published by St. Martin's Press, 175 Fifth Avenue, New York, NY 10010.

10 9 8 7 6 5 4 3 2 1

CONTENTS

Introduction

Well over half the attacks on human beings by sharks occur in water no more than five feet (1.5 metres) deep, according to statistical research.* This then begs a number of questions, including the following. How safe is it to go in the water at popular beach resorts around the coastlines of, for instance, the Mediterranean, the United States, South Africa, Hong Kong, Australia or even of Britain? Is the Atlantic coast of Florida as dangerous as California's Pacific waters? Is bathing in rivers safer than surfing, canoeing or diving? And if—heaven forbid—the next plane you take crashes into the sea, what are your chances of survival?

You may think you know the answers to such ghoulish questions, but the accounts of attacks presented in this book contain facts and events which will surprise all but the most sceptical and specialists in this field.

* H. D. Baldridge, *Shark Attack*, p. 108 (Everest, 1976)

"Let me die," pleaded the fourteen-year-old girl whose arm had been torn off while she bathed among a crowd on a beach in South Africa. "Shark, help!" screamed the English mother of quadruplets as she was ripped in half while diving off Tasmania. The holidaymaker on Malta, the Italian diver, the paddler in Florida, the fishermen left clinging to a raft in 1996, the Californian kayakers, the aircrash victims in the Gulf of Mexico, the boy in the river near Sydney, the elderly Hong Kong lady taking her daily dip, the Japanese shell fisherman—none of them was safe. Not even the two children playing at the edge of the water on an English south coast beach.

For most of us the fear of being attacked and eaten alive by an unseen monster who appears out of nowhere is a deep-seated one, but we try to dismiss such thoughts as irrational. "It couldn't happen to me," we would say to ourselves. As we grew up, we learned to discount the occasional horrifying rumour or sensational news story about sharks. Such unpleasant events occurred elsewhere, in exotic, far-away places, not at our local beaches or at our favourite holiday spot. We were confident it was safe to go in the water . . . And then came the blockbusting film based on Peter Benchley's novel *Jaws*—and our worst nightmares seemed to be confirmed. Or is this merely Hollywood hype?

Unfortunately it is not.

There are, in truth, fearsomely aggressive sharks over twenty feet long and weighing as much as a truck which attack boats and eat humans. However, like sensational tabloid headlines around the world, such bare, unqualified statements exaggerate our fears and fail to provide a balanced picture. After all, anyone reading this book probably stands more chance of being struck by lightning or of winning the top prize in a national lottery than of being bitten by a shark, let alone devoured by one. It may also prove comforting to recall that, in response to a question concerning the Royal Navy's need for an effective shark repellent during the Second World War, the then Prime Minister, Winston Churchill, declared forcefully to the House of Commons that "the British Government is entirely opposed to sharks!"

While seafarers the world over have, since time immemorial, feared "the monsters of the deep," the first reliable written accounts of seamen being killed by sharks did not appear until the sixteenth century. There is no suggestion, however, that such events were uncommon. In 1580 a sailor fell overboard from a storm-tossed sailing ship somewhere between Portugal and its destination in India. As the hapless man grasped the line thrown to him by his shipmates and was being hauled back towards the ship, a "large monster called tiburon" suddenly leapt from beneath the waves and "tore him to pieces before our very eyes. That surely was a grievous death."

Not long afterwards, in 1595, it was reported that:

This fish doth great mischiefe and devoureth many men that fish for pearles . . . As our ship lay in the River of Cochin [India] . . . it happened that as we were to hang on [replace] our rutter [rudder], . . . a saylor, being made fast with a corde to the ship, hung downe with halfe his body into the water to place the same [rudder] upon the hookes, and there came one of those Hayens [sharks] and bit one of his legs, to the middle of his thigh, cleane off at a bit[e], notwithstanding that the Master [ship's captain] stroke at him with an oare, and as the poor man was putting down his arms to feel his wound, the same Fish at the second time for another bit did bite off his hand and arme above the elbow, and also a peece of his buttocke.

Over subsequent centuries the perils of travelling by ship or in small vessels remained the same for seamen and passengers alike until the advent of the Second World War, when at last governments began to give serious consideration to the substantial loss of human life and the cost thereof. Between 1939 and 1945 thousands, perhaps hundreds of thousands, of men and women endured unimaginable horrors as they floated helplessly in the sea following the loss of their ship or plane owing to enemy action. The huge proportion of such people who were lost to shark attacks and the dreadful experiences recounted by survivors eventually forced naval authorities to investigate the possibility of developing shark repellents and other aids to survival.

Progress was slow, however. It was only in 1958, when prompted by memories of the losses suffered by such vessels as the USS *Indianapolis* in 1945 (see page 122) and the realization that no effective shark repellent was available, that the United States Office of Naval Research decided to fund a research programme related to sharks. That same year a group of international scientists met in New Orleans to discuss the problems involved. This, in turn, gave rise to the establishment of a Shark Research Panel, which agreed to co-ordinate the work and reports of international researchers. In addition, the panel initiated the Shark Attack File, the first attempt to document comprehensively shark attacks on a global historical basis. After undergoing various changes over the years, the file evolved into what is now known as the International Shark Attack File, based at the University of Florida in Gainesville under the auspices of the American Elasmobranch Society.

With the support of the Society, an international organization of scientists actively engaged in the study of sharks, skates, rays and chimaeras, and under the directorship of ichthyologist George Burgess, the File's growing data base and archive cover primarily North America, Australia, Hawaii and South Africa. By the start of 1996, the File had expanded to contain roughly 2,500 individual investigations of shark attacks worldwide.

Given the existence of such a file, one might imagine that information on the where, when and how of shark attacks would be readily available to interested enquirers, but this is not the case. The constraints of cost, time and insufficient manpower have resulted, it is suggested, in access being strictly limited to qualified scientists whose aims and research credentials are approved by the Society. In addition, access to the File is restricted because, in the words of its Director, it "contains much information that is considered privileged, such as medical reports, autopsies and personal interviews." However, the restriction on information seems to go well beyond such sensitive, confidential material.

The Director kindly responded to a request from this author by supplying, with admirable speed, the rather frustratingly vague figures for worldwide shark attacks reported to the File between 1990 and 1995 (given on p. 235). But, perhaps surprisingly, there has so far been only silence in response to this author's subsequent request for precise dates and rough locations (name of country) regarding shark attacks in the Mediterranean 1990–95.

Could it be that something other than a natural respect for the privacy of victims (including those connected with them) and the appropriateness of a researcher's academic qualifications plays a part in the decision on what information to release? Is there something "secret" about the date of an attack and the country where it occurred? Are not these bare facts in the interest of public safety and a matter of public record? After all, inhabitants in the region of an attack already know the whole story, and local papers generally publish a report, which anyone could unearth providing he or she had the necessary minimum facts plus the resources and tenacity to do so.

In the following pages, however, readers will discover much to enlighten, surprise and move them. The courage of survivors and of those who went to their aid is frequently awesome and inspiring. This book offers a wide selection of significant first-hand accounts and news reports of shark attacks around the world. While every effort has been made to make the text as comprehensive as possible, information emanating from Third World countries is sparse—in part because attacks may be too commonplace to be worthy of report—and in certain other areas of the world attacks are kept quiet for fear of damaging tourism through bad publicity.

Over the past fifteen years or so there has been a substantial increase in reports of shark attacks. The reasons for this are inevitably complex, but at least three factors seem to play a part. Firstly there is a growing number of people participating in marine sports and activities. Secondly coastal and marine pollution is growing, and this attracts the small fish on which many sharks feed to the shallows where humans disport themselves. Thirdly, where there is overfishing, sharks are being forced to seek new types of food. Above all, however, recent research indicates that, in much the same way as growling dogs bite postmen, sharks exhibit warning signals to "invaders" before launching an attack to protect what they perceive to be their territory or space. When humans go into or on to the sea, they enter the domain of the shark and do so at their own risk. It is not the shark's fault if he is driven to act aggressively. Guidance on how to avoid shark attacks and details concerning particular varieties of shark are largely beyond the scope of this publication, though valuable information may be gleaned from the stories which follow.

The first report in each chapter has been chosen for its drama or special interest. Subsequent accounts are presented in chronological order starting with the most recent attack. However, where several attacks are linked by shark or by area, those reports appear in order of occurrence. A full chronological list of attacks included in this book can be found on page 237.

Finally the author would like to acknowledge, with grateful thanks, the help of the following individuals and organizations: William Jennings, for valuable help in research; the staff of the British Library and its Newspaper Library at Colindale; George Burgess of the International Shark Attack File; Terry Mowschenson; Gaia Servadio; Jane and Nick Harding, and their Tasmanian relations; Marco Flagg; Bill Curtsinger and *National Geographic*; Simone Jorissen; David Sweetman; Richard Dodman, for suggesting the subject of shark attacks, Carol O'Brien, for signing me up, and all their supportive colleagues at Constable Publishers; and, last, but by no means least, Delphine MacCormick for her endless support and encouragement.

1
Holiday Snaps in the Shallows

Popular belief has it that British sharks are harmless. Tell that to the Scottish fisherman who was terribly mauled by a shark while he was fishing close inshore from his home port. Or the Devon skindiver who fought off a big Porbeagle shark that came into shallow water off Bee Sands in Devon. Or the parents of the two children who were playing in the shallows of a well-known south coast beach when they were knocked flying by an unprovoked attack from a pair of thresher sharks.

Fortunately for the bathing and boating public, the seas around our coasts have been rich enough in fish life to satisfy any shark. Times, however, are changing. The once prolific mackerel shoals that normally supply our sharks with the bulk of their food are being decimated so rapidly by commercial overfishing that the shark population is now being forced to look elsewhere for a readily available food supply.

The Times, London, 3 July 1976

HONG KONG, 1995

Hong Kong has suddenly found its attention turned from fears of the impending Chinese takeover to something even more terrifying—a spate of shark attacks [see list p. 235].

The latest attack, the third in two weeks, occurred yesterday at Clearwater Bay, an exclusive beachfront area of the city. Lifeguards pulled a forty-five-year-old woman out of shallow water where she had been swimming with fifty other people. Witnesses said one leg and one arm had been ripped off. She died before reaching hospital.

The attacks have confounded the politically correct view of sharks, that they are an unnecessarily victimised, environmentally friendly fish. Even Peter Benchley, author of *Jaws*, the man who did more than any other to besmirch the shark's reputation, has joined the revisionists. The post-modern, post-*Jaws* battle cry is: "Man eats more sharks than sharks eat man." But this argument is unlikely to find many adherents in Hong Kong just now.

A middle-aged swimmer said she heard the victim shouting for help with her hands raised above her. The woman then disappeared. "A pool of blood spilled out in the water, which was only up to her chest," the witness said.

Shark Attacks

The death of the woman—the third shark attack victim in a fortnight—was attributed to a possible feeding frenzy by a pack of sharks. No single species has yet been named as a suspect. But many people fear the beaches are being stalked by a large, lone killer with a taste for human flesh not too different from Mr. Benchley's celebrated protagonist.

Local experts think the same shark could be responsible for this year's attacks and other fatal attacks in recent years. In June 1993 a hair salon owner was killed while swimming in the same vicinity. Two weeks later another swimmer was killed.

Man may be ultimately responsible. Hong Kong beaches are notorious for their pollution. Garbage and sewage have been known to attract sharks. When the pollution clears, the garbage is replaced by tasty bathers.

Independent, London, 14 June 1995

SOMALIA, EAST AFRICA, 1993

The United Nations yesterday unveiled what may go down as its only success in the Somali capital, Mogadishu—an antishark net installed at a cost of £40,000 to protect UN workers on the main beach.

Shark attacks on the beach next to the international airport were unknown when hundreds of US Marines cavorted in the Indian Ocean. But, since the UN took over command of the international force in Somalia last May, three foreigners—a French woman, an American and a Russian—have been killed by sharks attracted by effluent from ships close to the shore.

The French woman was killed when she swam well out to sea, but the last two victims were taken in waist-deep water. Since then the beach has been closed.

Farouk Mawlawi, the UN spokesman in Mogadishu, yesterday defended the cost of the net and said it would be left "for the use of the Somalis" when the UN leaves.

The Times, London, 25 November 1993

HONG KONG, 1993

Stories about man-eating sharks sell newspapers from Australia to Hong Kong, and the creature or creatures that have devoured two people here in two weeks, and another two years ago, are dominating the colony's front pages.

"We stalk the killer," the *Standard*, the livelier of Hong Kong's two English language daily newspapers, declared yesterday. The *Standard* is sponsoring the visit here of Vic Hislop, a tiny Australian who is one of the world's most famous shark hunters. Mr. Hislop is a Crocodile Dundee–like character who wears a shark-tooth pendant, shorts and thongs. He has been busy for two days in his boat, flinging ducks and large fish into Silverstrand bay where Kwong Konghing, a furniture dealer, had his leg and hand bitten off in waist-deep water last Friday by a shark said to be more than eighteen feet long.

The Times, London, 15 June 1993

SANTA MARGHERITA LIGURE, ITALY, 1991

The Italian Riviera authorities have banned swimming at the height of the holiday season after a shark attacked a waterbed. Nobody was hurt. Greenpeace said the sighting had sparked unjustified hysteria, leading to "a senseless monster hunt."

Reuters, 2 August 1991

TEXAS, USA, 1987

A girl whose arm was bitten off by a shark remained hospitalized in a serious condition on Sunday, but officials said they will not close beaches to the thousands of Easter weekend visitors.

April Dawn Voglino, 16, of Kingsland, underwent surgery on Saturday at Memorial Medical Center in Corpus Christi, and was in the intensive care unit, nursing supervisor D. Brown said.

The teenager was in chest-deep water near Mustang Island on Saturday when the shark attacked her. She was swimming with her father, who pounded on the shark and carried her ashore after the shark swam away. Her arm was severed about six to eight inches above the elbow.

Nueces County Commissioner J. P. Luby, whose precinct covers two and a half miles of beaches, said the attack probably was an isolated case and he would not order the beaches closed.

Luby said he planned to fly over the area with Coast Guard officials to make observations of any sharks. The flight was delayed because of mechanical problems with the Coast Guard helicopter.

"We'll take some action if we see a lot of sharks out there," Luby said. "We've had people bitten before, but nothing as major as this."

Andre Landry, a fish behaviour expert from Texas A & M University at Galveston, said there have been between thirteen and fifteen documented shark attacks along the Texas coast within the last hundred years. "We have one incident happening like this and this arouses the concern of bathers, but it's a freak occurrence, something that should not induce fear among the bathing populace," Landry said on Sunday.

Luby said Voglino and her parents were alone at an isolated beach near Aransas Beach about 6 pm on Saturday when the attack occurred. Robert Voglino, who was swimming with his daughter, was not hurt, Luby said.

"The father heard the daughter scream and, as he turned around, he saw the daughter and the shark," Nueces County Constable Deewayne Mathews said. "He then headed directly toward his daughter. He grabbed the daughter and started beating on the shark with his other hand. At that time the shark severed the girl's arm."

Voglino continued to beat the shark and yelled at his daughter to swim to the shore, Mathews added. When the shark swam away, the father carried his daughter to shore. They flagged down a motorist who had a citizens' band radio and called for help.

New Orleans Times-Picayune, 20 April 1987

FLORIDA, USA, 1984

A twenty-three-year-old woman who was attacked by a shark while swimming just twenty feet off shore underwent surgery on Tuesday to repair a nine-inch gash in her right arm, a hospital official said.

Sunday's attack on Sandra Fletcher was the sixth to occur in a month along Florida's Atlantic coast.

Fletcher was in fair condition at Indian River Memorial Hospital before the operation, which was to reconnect severed nerves and tendons, and to stitch wounds made by the shark's double row of teeth.

"I knew what it was as soon as it grabbed me," she said on Monday from her hospital bed. "You always think it's something in the movies. You don't think it's going to happen to you."

Fletcher was attacked while body surfing with friends in waist-deep water three miles south of Sebastian Inlet in northern Indian River County. "I just saw all the blood in the water. I thought I was going to get it again. I was scared," the Clearwater teacher said.

Karen Kenney, 27, of Tampa, was with Fletcher

and helped the injured woman pull herself free. "As soon as Sandy screamed, I saw blood in the wave behind her," Kenney said. "I ran out and tried to help pull her in. He just pulled her under—she had to fight to get loose. When she screamed, you could see a trail of blood in the water about five feet wide."

"She was very lucky that it didn't hit the major artery or she probably wouldn't have made it," Dr. Peter Ciejek said. He described the gash on Fletcher's right forearm at nine to twelve inches long.

Six shark attacks have been reported in the past month between Stuart and Daytona Beach along Florida's east coast. Indian River County lifeguard Bruce Little said shark sightings are common at this time of year because "bait fish like mullet are migrating south now and the sharks follow them. It's dangerous to swimmers when the bait fish come too close to shore."

New Orleans Times-Picayune, 24 October 1984

TEXAS, USA, 1984

A teenage girl's legs were mangled by bites from a shark while another girl required seventy stitches to close bite wounds, but city officials decided to keep their popular beaches open. "We're probably taking more precautions than necessary," said city official Joe Rubio.

Carmen Gaytan, 18, attacked in the Gulf of Mexico by what rescuers said was a four-foot shark, was in guarded condition yesterday in the intensive care unit of Valley Community Hospital. She underwent extensive reconstructive surgery on her legs. "It's just wait and see," hospital spokeswoman Suzy Payne said of Gaytan's chances to recover without an amputation.

The second teenage girl was attacked just two and a half hours later in front of another luxury hotel three miles away and required stitches on many leg bites, authorities said.

City and tourism officials met and decided to keep the beaches open following the attacks, described as the first in the area in twenty-three years. The beaches were kept under surveillance by land, sea and air, said Rubio, a South Padre Island building department official who acts as city spokesman in emergencies. He said beaches in this South Padre Island resort at the southern tip of Texas would be evacuated if "any suspicious activity that can be confirmed as sharks" is spotted.

Gary Glick, who owns a deep-sea fishing charterboat in Port Isabel, said shifts in ocean currents moved sharks closer to the shore . . .

Gaytan, of Mexico, was swimming in chest-deep water shortly after noon on Tuesday outside the South Padre Hotel when beachgoers heard her screams for help. "Help me please, a fish is killing me," she cried, according to Cidonio Barron Leon, who helped pull her out. He said he saw a shark as he went to her aid.

The second attack, on a thirteen-year-old girl whose identity was not released yesterday, occurred near the Tiki Motel about two and a half hours later, officials said. The girl was treated at the Port Isabel

Medical Center and was released, Dr. Ralph Landberg said. "She had lots of teeth marks around her right foot up to her ankle. There were many lacerations," said Landberg, adding that the girl took seventy stitches. "I think she was very lucky."

However, Rubio said there was no evidence the second girl had been attacked by a shark. "We're not sure what happened," he said.

Mid-July is the height of the summer season for the high-rise hotels and condominiums on South Padre Island. No cancellations or early checkouts were reported by clerks at the two hotels where the attacks occurred.

New Orleans Times-Picayune, 26 July 1984

VIRGINIA, USA, 1983

A fourteen-year-old girl who had a chunk taken from her foot and leg while swimming in the Atlantic apparently was attacked by a sand shark, authorities said. Jill Redenbaugh was in satisfactory condition on Tuesday at a Virginia Beach hospital after undergoing surgery on Monday.

She was swimming in waist-deep water twenty to thirty feet from the shore when she was attacked, police said.

Jack Kownsend, who helped the girl, said "a two-inch chunk" of her left foot and Achilles tendon was taken out.

Kownsend and Ernest Singleton helped Redenbaugh out of the water. Singleton wrapped her foot and took her to the hospital. "She was a very brave young lady," Singleton said. "She held herself together very well. The emergency room physician thought it might have been a sand shark."

Harris Stewart Jr., director of the Center for Marine Studies at Old Dominion University, said sand sharks grow to six feet long and generally live in shallow water near sandy bottoms. "They terrify you, but the incidence of their giving you trouble are few and far between," Stewart said. "Usually you can scare a sand shark away by going 'Boo.' "

It was only the third shark attack at Virginia Beach recorded in twenty-seven years. In 1973 a shark bit a seventeen-year-old boy crabbing at False Cape. In 1956 a fourteen-year-old girl was attacked by a shark while she was swimming.

New Orleans Times-Picayune, 17 August 1983

FLORIDA, USA, 1981

"All I could see was teeth. I was so scared, I just started slapping him," Van Horn Ely, Florida's fifteenth reported shark attack victim of the year, recalled.

Ely, 19, underwent five hours of surgery on his left hand and arm, badly mauled in a shark attack which occurred only about thirty feet from shore in waist-deep water. The attack occurred on Monday, just three days after Robert Kiefling, 17, of Cocoa, was bitten on the left foot while surfing in the water off Cocoa Beach. Two earlier shark victims—Mark

Meeker, 26, attacked in Tampa Bay, and Christy Wapniarski, 19, attacked off Ormond Beach (see p. 156)—bled to death.

"I've swum from Maine to the Caribbean and a lot of places in between and never even known anyone who was bothered by sharks," said Ely, who moved to Jupiter Island four days ago from Cape May, New Jersey, to take a job as maintenance man at the Jupiter Island Beach Club.

Ely was attacked when he went for a swim in the Atlantic during his lunch break. He estimated the shark that seized his hand and forearm was six to eight feet in length. "It all happened in just a second or so," Ely said. "He bit down pretty hard. He pulled me, took me forward. I tried to slide my hand out of his mouth. His mouth was out of the water. All I could see was teeth. I was so scared, I just started slapping at him."

Somehow Ely managed to tug his hand free and turn and run through the water toward the shore. "I was most worried that he was going to come back and bite my leg. I didn't have much trouble running back to shore," he said.

As he ran to shore, he shouted to a youth on the beach in a golf cart, who stopped, picked him up and drove him to the Jupiter Island police station. Officers swathed his lacerated hand and arm in a towel and called an ambulance to take him to a hospital, where surgeons completed repair of his hand and arm after 5 am on Tuesday.

The unusually high number of attacks this year has been blamed by some shark experts on the abnormal warmth of Atlantic waters. As a result, they say, schools of smelt fish, such as mullet, have been feeding close to shore and sharks, which prey on the schools, have been attracted closer than usual to Florida's beaches.

The experts say sharks have notoriously bad eyesight and most attacks on humans are cases of mistaken identity. They mistake a hand or foot for a fish, particularly if the swimmer is close to a school of bait fish.

New Orleans Times-Picayune, 21 October 1981

PERTH, AUSTRALIA, 1969

A fifteen-year-old Sea Scout who was attacked by a shark in seven feet of water in the Swan River yesterday said today he had used one foot to push the shark away after it had mauled his other leg.

"After I had been bitten I was scared that the shark might strike again," Graham Cartwright of Mettam Street, Trigg, said from his bed in the Royal Perth Hospital today. "He took two chomps and that was it. I felt his rough skin with my hands and one eye as I pushed him away with my good foot.

"I called out: 'Help, help—a shark's got me' during a 400-yard swim from the other side of the river. My best friend, Greg Hams, was nearly at the shore when he heard me call. He yelled out to John, who had just reached the river's edge."

John Brockmeulen, 14, of Mt. Lawley, called out to some boys to get an ambulance and then swam out to Graham.

"He told me to turn over on to my back and towed

13

me ashore. I was all right in the water, but could not bear to look at my leg once I was ashore," said Graham.

Graham was bleeding profusely from a four-inch deep tear in his left thigh as he was towed 100 yards to shore.

Pathologist Graeme Shute, a scoutmaster in the 1st Mt. Lawley Sea Scouts, stemmed the flow of blood. The wound extended from the knee upwards and had opened the flesh on the inside of the boy's thigh. There were one-and-a-half-inch teeth marks in a nine-inch radius.

John Brockmeulen said he thought Graham had scared the shark away by sheer luck when he touched one of its sensitive eyes. "I was confident I would not be attacked by the shark because I had read that a second person was not usually attacked," he said.

Surgeons operated on Graham's mauled leg for five hours on Saturday night. They expect him to regain the full use of it. He should be in hospital for a week.

Graham, a Balcatta High School student and keen surfer, who was to have started his end-of-term examinations today, said he did not think he would swim in the river again. "But the ocean will be OK," he said.

The three boys were among a group of twenty Sea Scouts who had spent the afternoon sailing and scouting. The attack took place thirteen miles upstream.

Sydney Morning Herald, 1 December 1969

NAPLES, ITALY, 1966

Bathers along the Gulf of Naples were warned today not to swim beyond 400 yards from the shore because of the danger of sharks. A Coast Guard cutter yesterday sighted a number of sharks in the gulf, a relatively rare event. Today fishermen and maritime police were patrolling the area.

The Times, London, 14 June 1966

SYDNEY, AUSTRALIA, 1963

Miss Marcia Hathaway, a well-known Sydney actress, was fatally mauled by a shark in Middle Harbour yesterday afternoon. The shark attacked her while she was standing in murky water only thirty inches deep and twenty feet from the shore in the northern arm of Sugarloaf Bay.

Seconds before she died, while friends were hurrying her to hospital, Miss Hathaway told her fiancé, "I am not in pain. Don't worry about me, dear. God will look after me."

Miss Hathaway, 32, of Greenway Flats, Milson's Point, was on a picnic trip with six friends in a motor cruiser.

When the shark attacked, her fiancé, who was beside her, fought the shark with his hands and kicked it as it twisted in the blood-stained water, trying to drag its victim into deep water.

Miss Hathaway died twenty minutes later from her terrible injuries and shock. The shark almost tore off her right leg. Miss Hathaway's fiancé and two other friends were treated at the Mater Misericordiae Hospital for shock.

Miss Hathaway and her fiancé, Frederick Knight, 38, a journalist of Cook Street, Double Bay, were in the party of seven holidaying on the twenty-eight-foot cabin cruiser *Valeeta*.

Knight said later that Miss Hathaway at first thought she had been attacked by an octopus. "I have seen men die, but I have never seen anyone so brave as Marcia," he said. "I think the last words she said to me were, 'Don't worry about me, dear, God will look after me.' When I asked her if it hurt much, she said, 'No, I am not in pain.' She was a very religious girl. We were to announce our engagement formally on her birthday, Friday the 8th.

"I did not get a close look at the shark, I saw a fin and its girth as I straddled it. My legs were wide apart and its body touched both of them."

The *Valeeta* was anchored about twenty yards from where the shark attacked, which was close to shore. The attack occurred in a small bay with a small watercourse at its head. Several homes back on to the water about 700 yards away; they are not visible from the beach.

The other members of the party were David Mason, 28, a journalist, and Peter Cowden, 27, both of Balmain, who are joint owners of the cruiser, James

Delmege, 39, of Potts Point, Alan Simpson, 21, of Auburn, and Sandra Hayden, 19, of Blacktown. Mason, Cowden and Simpson were on the *Valeeta*, Delmege and Miss Hayden were only about three or four feet from the shore gathering oysters from the rocks, while Knight and Miss Hathaway were standing in shallow water about twenty feet out.

Knight said, when the shark attacked, he was only a few feet away from Miss Hathaway. "I went to her and tried to drag her from the shark. It seemed like ten minutes to me while we struggled, but it could only have been a couple of minutes. The water was stained with blood and I never thought I would get her away from it. I think at one stage I had my foot in its mouth. It felt soft and spongy. I'm not too clear what happened. It happened so fast and I could not see much in the water. I tried to reassure her and told her that the shark had just brushed past her, but she knew a short time after that she was dying."

Delmege said he had his back to the couple when the shark attacked. Sandra Hayden was a few feet away from him. "I heard a scream, looked around and thought they were just skylarking. I continued looking for oysters," he said. "Then I heard a second scream and I turned, and saw the water bloodstained and foaming. I dashed in and helped Fred Knight to get Marcia away from the shark."

Knight said the shark apparently attacked Miss Hathaway below the calf on the right leg, then in a second lunge embedded its teeth into her upper right thigh near the hip. Her right leg was almost torn off.

Delmege and Knight carried Miss Hathaway to

the sandy beach in the small cove. Mason said that, when he and Cowden saw the attack, they tore sheets off the cruiser's bunks for tourniquets, then rowed to shore in the dinghy. They applied tourniquets on the beach, lifted Miss Hathaway into the dinghy and rowed back to the *Valeeta*. They took the cruiser to a boatshed at the foot of Edinburgh Road, Castlecrag, where Knight dived overboard and swam about twenty yards to a house to get the occupants to phone for an ambulance.

He swam back to the cruiser and comforted his fiancée as they made for Mowbray Point, where they were met by ambulance officers Ray Wrightson and Robert Smith of Central District Ambulance. Miss Hathaway was unconscious. The ambulancemen used oxygen in an attempt to revive her.

They put her in an ambulance, but, because of the steep grade leading up from the water's edge and slippery surface, the ambulance clutch burnt out. Although about thirty people, including Knight, tried desperately to push the vehicle, the gradient was too steep. A reporter radioed his office and a second ambulance was sent.

Ambulance officers worked on Miss Hathaway continuously and doctors at the hospital also tried to revive her, but she was dead. Miss Hathaway's mother collapsed when told the news of her death and was taken by ambulance to a private hospital.

Mr. Michael Vaux, the owner of the Castlecrag boatshed, where the *Valeeta* pulled in with Miss Hathaway, said he saw two large sharks earlier in the morning in the bay. "There were a couple of dogs taken by sharks in the area last week," he said.

Sydney Morning Herald, 29 January 1963

MACKAY, AUSTRALIA, 1961

Doctors are fighting desperately to save the life of eighteen-year-old Margaret Hobbs, a victim of yesterday's shark attack at Mackay.

Miss Hobbs has been receiving continuous transfusions of blood and saline solutions since she was admitted to the Mater Hospital, Mackay, at 3 pm yesterday. She is dangerously ill. Late tonight her condition was unchanged.

Miss Hobbs, a schoolteacher of Owen's Creek, near Mackay, and a friend, Martyn Steffens, 24, of Brisbane, were mauled by the shark as they stood in waist-deep water at Lambert's Beach.

Doctors in a two-hour emergency operation last night amputated Miss Hobbs' right leg near the hip. Her right arm was torn off at the shoulder and her left arm torn off above the wrist.

Steffens had his right hand and wrist mauled. Doctors amputated his hand above the wrist. His condition tonight was serious, but doctors consider his progress satisfactory.

Graham Jorgensen, 27, who saved the couple by driving the shark away, said today the couple had entered the water to wash sand off their bodies after playing on the beach. When the attack occurred, he was sitting on the beach with the rest of the party . . .

Evidence of a growing shark menace in eastern Australian waters came with reports of shark sightings yesterday in many areas: a ten-foot shark surfaced near a fisherman while he was swimming to safety from a burning, sinking trawler off Southport, Queensland; a shark snapped a fish from a fisherman's line as he stood in shallow water near Murwillumbah; the body of a drowned man mauled by a shark was found yesterday floating in the Brisbane river; and a shark swam within ten feet of four adults and nine children at Northcliffe, south of Surfers' Paradise, on Thursday.

Sydney Morning Herald, 30 December 1961

Margaret Hobbs, 18, the Mackay shark victim, died at 6:30 last night. Her death ended a grim round-the-clock battle by doctors and nurses since the attack. A sister at the Mater Hospital said, "Miss Hobbs fought courageously for her life."

Miss Hobbs lost consciousness in the afternoon and her parents were called to her bedside. Friends later took them home. "They couldn't stand it any longer," a hospital sister said. A doctor was called urgently in the late afternoon, but Miss Hobbs gradually sank.

A hospital sister who was with Miss Hobbs almost continually said tonight, "There was never any real hope. Margaret just held her own for the first twenty-four hours, but her condition deteriorated overnight and it was never good at any time today. She knew her parents this morning and was able to say 'yes,' 'Mum' and 'Dad'—that's all. Margaret was very brave and she was fighting until the moment she lost consciousness."

Sisters at the hospital said that Martyn Steffens had been told during the day that Margaret's condition was deteriorating. His mother and her father were with him when the news of her death was broken to him at 7:15 pm. Friends of the couple said Steffens went to Mackay just before Christmas to meet the Hobbs family before announcing his engagement to Margaret.

More than twenty shark alarms along Queensland's central coast sent swimmers scattering from the water yesterday.

At Pacific Beach, near Surfers' Paradise, a group of fishermen digging for worms in ankle-deep water fled as a ten-foot shark cruised past in two feet of water less than ten feet away.

North Burleigh Beach lifesavers closed the beach three times in four hours when sharks nosed in close to swimmers. All lifesaving clubs from the Gold Coast to the far north maintained doubled patrols, but many swimmers stayed out of the water or remained in the shallows. A privately owned spotting aircraft will keep a tight watch for sharks at the Yeppoon to Emu Park beaches. The aircraft's pilot today saw sharks up to ten feet long cruising within three yards of swimmers.

Sydney Sun-Herald, 31 December 1961

NATAL, SOUTH AFRICA, 1957

Doctors and nurses at Port Shepstone Hospital were still fighting early today to save the life of Julia Painting, a fourteen-year-old Bulawayo girl mauled by a shark as she bathed among hundreds of visitors at Margate yesterday. At midnight her condition was reported as "unchanged." Her left arm was torn off and flesh savaged from her body.

She murmured, "Let me die," as she was being taken to hospital. Julia was later reported to be still in a serious condition, but "there is a very slight improvement." She was operated on soon after the attack—the fourth since 19 December 1957 on the Natal South Coast. Her life hung in the balance when it was learnt that the hospital's blood bank was empty. Nurses and hospital staff immediately volunteered to be bled and, while two pints were being collected, an urgent call for ten pints of blood was sent to the hospital at Renishaw. It arrived in time.

The Margate Town Council banned all bathing off the beach until further notice at a special meeting held after the attack on Julia. Bathing will be allowed in the lagoon as soon as it has been deepened and the mouth sandbagged. The Council also decided to erect a shark net immediately.

A large crowd on the beach heard Julia's screams for help. They watched in horrified silence as the shark wrestled with her in clear, knee-deep water about thirty yards from the beach. Two men, Mr. Paul Brokensha, 36, of Fort Victoria, Rhodesia, and a Margate lifesaver, Mr. Aubrey Cowan, fought to free Julia from the shark's jaws. Eventually the shark let go and swam away.

Julia was standing in unclouded water on the fringe of hundreds of other bathers when the shark made its savage attack, taking away her left arm and leaving lacerations on her chest. A dumbfounded crowd of more than 2,000 on the beach heard the first frantic warning screams of "shark" and watched as the flurried water became blood red.

Lifesavers jumped to action and sounded a warning siren. Only moments previously a spotter aircraft of the shark patrol had passed over the area before wheeling back towards St. Michael's.

Julia, her fifteen-year-old nephew Laurie, an uncle, Mr. Arthur Painting, and Mr. Brokensha were having a final dip before leaving the surf. Julia was due to return home today. She had been on holiday with her uncle and aunt for a month.

Mr. Brokensha described how, standing only a few yards from Julia, he saw, simultaneously with her, the shark moving in to the first attack. It went straight for her without turning on its side. With a savage thrust it hit her and immediately mauled her side, before wheeling around for a second attack.

Mr. Brokensha caught the shark's tail and tried to drag Julia away, but her costume came away in his hands. He started raining blows on the shark's back, but, in his own words, "It was like punching very solid leather and there was no 'give' at all."

The shark was so powerful that, with a flick of its tail, it threw him off. He immediately returned to the fray and hit the shark again. The shark let go, but not until it had severed the girl's arm at the shoulder and severely savaged her body.

The attack was so sudden and unexpected that the four lifesavers realized that a shark was in the water only when they heard horrified screams and saw the water churning beneath flaying fins. Mr. Frank Shephard, the Durban fishing authority, said that, from the description, the shark was undoubtedly a ragged-tooth shark—one of the most dangerous, and a cunning and quiet scavenger which creeps along the bottom towards the shore.

Cape Times, 31 December 1957

NATAL, SOUTH AFRICA, 1958

The increasing prevalence of attacks on human beings has led the Natal authorities to declare war on two kinds of pests—sharks and crocodiles.

The shark menace has grown alarmingly at bathing beaches at Natal South Coast resorts, where tens of thousands of visitors are now on summer holiday. In the past two weeks two youths have died after being attacked [see pp. 162–166], another youth had a leg bitten off, and a fourteen-year-old girl is in a critical condition after her arm was torn off and other parts of her body mutilated. All these attacks occurred in shallow water near the beach in the presence of large numbers of other bathers. Helicopters and light aircraft have been engaged on a shark-spotting patrol on this stretch of the coast, and a South African naval minesweeper has now been ordered to the area to lay depth charges.

In the northern Natal territory of Zululand crocodiles have been making frequent attacks on human beings. The outcry against protection of these creatures reached a climax after the fourteen-year-old son of a Johannesburg doctor was killed while fishing on the bank of a lake. The provincial authorities have now decided to shoot out all crocodiles. Professional hunters and game wardens have been ordered to shoot crocodiles on sight, and local farmers have been asked to cooperate. Victims of crocodile attacks include both Europeans and Africans.

The Times, London, 3 January 1958

NATAL, SOUTH AFRICA, 1958

As a wave of horror swept Natal's South Coast after a fresh shark killing yesterday, at least three families decided to pack up and leave. Some visitors said that the South Coast would become a "ghost resort" if immediate steps were not taken to make bathing safe.

The victim of the latest attack, Mr. Derryet Garth Prinsloo, a forty-two-year-old farmer of Theunissen, Free State, was standing in about thirty inches of water a few yards from the shore and talking to a woman companion when he was taken by a lazy-grey shark at Scottburgh.

His frantic scream, "Help me, for God's sake help me," electrified the small crowd of early morning bathers as the shark, attacking from behind, ripped the flesh from both his legs and buttocks in a series of lightning attacks. As three rescuers pulled him from the surf on to the beach, his sixteen-year-old son, Jacques, rushed from the water and, cradling the head of his dying father in his lap, cried, "Daddy, Daddy, don't leave me. I'm with you. Please speak to me."

Mr. Prinsloo was taken to Renishaw Hospital in a station wagon, but was dead on arrival. An immediate ban was imposed by order of the Town Board on further bathing.

Mr. A. Laing of Boksburg and his twelve-year-old son, Neville, had been standing alongside Mr. Prinsloo only minutes before the attack. Mr. Laing, feeling the debris of washed cane from the river stroking his legs in the murky surf, said to his son, "This is shark water, let's get out."

While walking out of the surf, he heard the screams for help and, looking round, saw the shark lashing its tail in a flurry of blood-stained water. He rushed back to help Mr. I. Kelly of Ermelo and Mr. J. A. C. Nieman of Virginia, who were pulling Mr. Prinsloo by the arms away from the shark, which had knocked him on to his side. When they hauled him to the shore, both legs had been stripped of all flesh and the left leg was almost severed.

Mrs. Nieman, who, with her husband and two children, had gone for an early morning bathe with Mr. Prinsloo and his son, said she was standing right next to Mr. Prinsloo when the attack occurred. "He was saying, 'This is what I like about the waves here—they're so beautifully even.' They were his last words. The next thing I knew he was screaming for help."

Mr. D. Stamatis of Scottburgh, an experienced shark fisherman, sent home for a shotgun after the attack. He took up a position on the rocks, from where he saw a shark—which he believed was a five-foot, 200lb lazy grey—make two more sorties into the shallow surf before 8:30 am.

Cape Times, 10 January 1958

NATAL, SOUTH AFRICA, 1958

A twenty-nine-year-old bather was killed by a large shark which attacked him repeatedly yesterday while his wife and two children watched horrified at Port Edward, one hundred miles south of here. A middle-aged African dived into the surf and dragged him out of the shark's jaws after a tug-of-war.

The man, Mr. Nicholas Francois Badenhorst, was dead when he was dragged to the beach by the African, Maseke, who plunged into the surf after frenzied appeals both from the victim and his brother, Andries Badenhorst, who was bathing with him.

The shark ripped off Mr. Badenhorst's left arm completely and took off his right arm below the elbow. It then mauled his abdomen and one of his legs.

Mr. Andries Badenhorst said last night: "My brother and I and an acquaintance were bathing a little way out—about chest-deep in the water. There were a lot of other bathers nearer the shore. Suddenly I saw this big shark. It was from ten to fifteen feet long. It attacked my brother. He yelled and I yelled. I think a line was sent out. A Native came in and pulled my brother out, but it was too late then. The water was all discoloured with blood."

Mr. Nicholas Badenhorst's children, who were on the beach with their mother, are five years and twenty months old. The family was staying at a holiday camp here. Mr. Badenhorst was a clerk on the

South African Railways, living at Sir George Grey Avenue, Horison, Roodepoort. Arrangements were immediately made to take the family to Durban, where they boarded the train which left for the Transvaal last night.

The attack was the sixth on the South Coast since December. Before 18 December, when sixteen-year-old Bob Wherley lost a leg at Karrideene, there had been no shark attacks in Natal waters since 1954. Then in quick succession came attacks at Uvongo beach, where Alan Green, 14, was killed (see p. 162) only twenty-four hours after the attack on Wherley, at Margate, where Vernon Berry (see p. 164), aged twenty-three, was killed on 23 December, and fourteen-year-old Julia Painting (see p. 21) lost her left arm and was mutilated a week later, and at Scottburgh, where Mr. D. G. Prinsloo, 42, was killed (see. p. 25) on 9 January.

The mayors of three of the South Coast's premier holiday resorts, Mr. Robert Barton (Margate), Mr. Arthur Howes (Amanzimtoti) and Mr. Les Payn (Scottburgh) last night appealed to holidaymakers to obey the bathing instruction of lifesavers. Mr. Barton said the tragedies indicated the danger of swimming outside safe-bathing enclosures. All three mayors pointed out that resort municipalities had spent thousands of pounds and many hours of deliberation in planning the safest form of bathing.

Cape Times, 4 April 1958

NATAL, SOUTH AFRICA, 1958

Efforts have been initiated to set up a statutory co-ordinating body to deal with the shark menace in South African coastal waters.

This move follows two more fatal attacks in shallow surf on Natal's south coast during the Easter holiday weekend. In one case a twenty-nine-year-old visitor, Mr. N. F. Badenhorst, was attacked while bathing in full view of his wife and two children.

In the second case Mrs. Fay Bester, 28, a widow with four young children, was attacked and killed in shallow surf. Three other bathers have been killed on this stretch of coast during the present summer season. An emergency meeting of the Natal Safety Bathing Association is to be held tomorrow to form a plan for coordinating anti-shark measures.

The Times, London, 8 April 1958

SYDNEY, AUSTRALIA, 1955

A man was killed by a fourteen-foot tiger shark in Sugarloaf Bay, Castlecrag, yesterday afternoon.

The man, Bruno Aloysius Rautenberg, a twenty-five-year-old German migrant, was attacked twice in about fifteen feet of water between fifteen and twenty yards from the shore. The shark tore Rautenberg's legs to pieces. The flesh on the left leg was torn off between the knee and the foot. Large pieces of flesh were bitten on the right leg.

Yesterday's shark fatality, the second in Sydney in three weeks, occurred at about 2 pm.

Rautenberg, a metalworker, boarded with Mr. and Mrs. K. Wood in Edinburgh Road, Castlecrag. He was cleaning himself in the bay after helping to clean out the Woods' swimming pool when the shark attacked. The attack was in a lonely part of Sugarloaf Bay, at the bottom of a high, sloping cliff.

Mr. Wood, 37, a clerk, said that after he and Rautenberg cleaned out the pool, which is built of rock, Rautenberg said he would wash the mud off himself in the bay. "I warned him not to go out far, but he said he would try and recover an anchor we lost a few days ago. Suddenly I heard him give a piercing scream. He was a very good swimmer, but I thought he was in difficulties. I ran to the bank near him. There was blood in the water all around him. The shark was right beside him. I saw the shark grab him by the leg, drag him under and hang on.

"I didn't think the shark would let his leg go. Neither my wife nor I can swim. We were the only people around. I grabbed a piece of water pipe about fifteen foot long and threw it at the shark to try and drive it off. By this time Rautenberg was so weak he couldn't do anything.

"When he came to the surface again I waded out a little way from the rock, grasped his body and carried him up the bank. He was dead when I got him ashore. My wife called the police and ambulance."

Mr. Wood said the shark seemed to have a pointed nose. It was black along the back. "It had a high triangular fin on its back," he said. "It was more than twice as long as Rautenberg. After the attack the shark swam around for more than two hours and I saw it six times during that time.

"Rautenberg migrated to Australia from Germany and had been boarding with us for about two months. He worked at Alexandria. He never spoke much about himself, but he told my wife he had a little girl, aged five, in Germany. He wanted the child and her mother to come to Australia and had been saving up for their fare. As far as we know, they were not very keen on coming out here."

Central District Ambulance officers and Dr. E. Manuel of Castlecrag hurried to the scene soon after the attack, but Rautenberg was dead. Police said they thought he died within about two minutes of the first attack because he lost so much blood.

Police and ambulance men had to make their way down hundreds of steps, through thick bush, to reach the scene. They said the arteries had been torn out of Rautenberg's legs and it would have been impossible to save his life.

Police said that the risk of shark attacks was high at present because the water temperature along the coast was about 74°F. They said this high temperature was bringing scores of sharks and big game fish into the harbour.

On 13 January John Willis, 13, was killed by a twelve-foot grey nurse shark while spearfishing off Balmoral Beach. On 1 March last year a shark mauled a lifesaver swimming alone at The Entrance, near Gosford. The lifesaver died three days later. There have been more than thirty-two fatal shark attacks in New South Wales since 1919. Yesterday's fatality was the eighth in Sydney Harbour since that same year . . . Six species of sharks in New South Wales waters are regarded as maneaters: the tiger, grey nurse, blue pointer or mako, white shark, black or bronze whaler and the hammerhead.

Sydney Sun-Herald, 6 February 1955

SYDNEY, AUSTRALIA, 1942

Zieta Steadman, 28, single, of Ashfield was killed by a shark while she was standing in shallow water in an upper part of Middle Harbour yesterday afternoon.

Miss Steadman was so shockingly mutilated that only the upper part of her body could be recovered. The remains were dragged from the jaws of the shark by Mr. Frederick H. Bowes of Charlotte Street, Ashfield. Mr. Bowes estimates that the shark was fourteen feet long.

Miss Steadman was a member of a picnic party, the other members of which were Mr. and Mrs. Bowes, and Mrs. Reeve, the elderly mother of Mrs. Bowes. They hired a motor launch from the boatshed of Mr. J. H. West in Sailor's Bay at 1:30 pm and travelled up Middle Harbour until they were about three and a half miles above the Spit Bridge. The boat was tied to a rock on the first point on the French's Forest shore past Bantry Bay, a locality near the power works which is known to fishermen as Egg Rock. The picnic party then had lunch on the rocky ledge which lies between the water and the steep hill above the harbour.

Close to the shore the water is shallow. It falls away slightly for about twenty-five feet and then drops steeply to a depth of thirty feet. There is no beach, the bottom being of shells and rocks. The water is clear. Shortly before three o'clock Mr. and Mrs. Bowes and Miss Steadman entered the water to bathe, while Mrs. Reeve watched them from an elevated position on the shore.

Mr. and Mrs. Bowes were standing together in water waist high. Miss Steadman was ten to twelve feet further out and in slightly deeper water. Mr. Bowes called to her not to go so far, and she turned to come back. Suddenly she threw out her arms and cried in terror. Simultaneously Mrs. Reeve saw the shark attacking her. Mrs. Reeve immediately screamed out to her son-in-law.

Mr. Bowes grabbed an oar from the boat and endeavoured to drive away the shark, which, in repeated attacks on Miss Steadman, was throwing itself out of the water and lashing the surface with its tail. The shark was so large that Mr. Bowes could make no impression on it with the oar.

Gradually the shark drew its victim toward deeper water. Mr. Bowes jumped into the boat, started the engine and steered the boat at the shark, every detail of which could be seen as it came to the surface, with the intention of ramming it. This plan failed. Mr. Bowes then circled in the boat and, as he again came closer to the young woman, he left the tiller, jumped to the side of the boat and grabbed her by her long black hair. It was obvious, however, that she was dead.

Mr. Bowes, a man of fifteen stone, had to use all his strength to free the upper portion of the body. So great was the force he had to exert that the young woman's hair bit into his hands. He saw the remainder of the body disappear into deep water. Mr. Bowes then placed the remains of Miss Steadman, covered by a piece of canvas, in the bottom of the boat. When the party returned to the boatshed, the ambulance and police were called.

Mr. West, owner of the boatshed, said last night that Mr. Bowes had behaved with courage and great coolness in one of the most terrible situations in which any man could be placed. "There was no help available. The only other men in sight were fishing from another boat which was hundreds of yards away. When they came along the whole terrible affair was over."

Sydney Morning Herald, 5 January 1942

SYDNEY, AUSTRALIA, 1942

Denise Rosemary Burch, 15, of Cliff Street, Manly, was taken by a whaler shark in two feet of water in Middle Harbour on Saturday morning. She died before she was lifted from the water.

Miss Burch was one of a party of four girls and four boys, including the dead girl's elder sister, Pamela. They left the Spit at about 9 am in two boats for a day's outing in Middle Harbour. The boys and girls, aged from fifteen to eighteen, rowed to Ironstone Point, near Bantry Bay, where they landed for lunch.

While one or two of the boys swam in deeper water, Miss Burch paddled in the shallow water. At about 10 am the girl was standing in about two feet of water when the other members of the party heard her scream. One of the boys was swimming about fifteen or twenty yards away in deep water. Miss Burch was seized by the legs and dragged under the water by the shark. For a minute or two neither the girl nor the shark could be seen, but the water was stained with blood.

One of the boys grabbed an oar, with which he tried to drive off the shark. Other members of the party joined him, armed with sticks and stones. A few moments later Miss Burch appeared above water. She was taken ashore by her companions. She had suffered terrible injuries and she was dead before the party reached the shore. The body was taken to the Spit, and Sergeant van Wouwe and Constable C. Fenton of the Water Police met the party.

Mrs. Burch and her two daughters were among those evacuated from Hong Kong about two years ago. Her husband, Mr. R. J. Burch, and their son are prisoners of war in the hands of the Japanese.

Sydney Morning Herald, 28 December 1942

SYDNEY, AUSTRALIA, 1935

A youth of twenty, while swimming across the Georges River, near Sydney, was attacked by a shark and so severely injured in the leg that he died from loss of blood.

Three hours later a girl of thirteen was attacked and her right arm and left hand were practically severed. It is believed that a tiger shark about five feet in length was responsible for both attacks. The girl's condition is critical.

The Times, London, 1 January 1935

NEW SOUTH WALES, AUSTRALIA, 1922

Sir Walter Davidson, Governor of New South Wales, is sending an official report to the King [George V] of a gallant attempt by a returned soldier, Jack Chalmers, to rescue a boy named Coghlan from the jaws of a shark, with a recommendation that the Albert Medal be awarded to Chalmers, for whom a large sum of money has been collected locally.

The Times, London, 15 February 1922

DEVON, UNITED KINGDOM, 1919

A shark which had made its appearance among women bathers at Croyde, North Devon, on Tuesday was the cause of considerable excitement. The bathers got safely ashore, and the shark was shot by Mr. C. C. Cuff, assistant manager in the Great Western locomotive works, Swindon. It took five persons to drag ashore the shark, which measured 7ft 6 in. in length.

The Times, London, 14 August 1919

2
Down into the Deep

TUSCANY, ITALY, 1989

The shark hunt is on. In the usually peaceful waters off the coast of Tuscany a small army of amateurs and professionals are searching for a twenty-foot killer shark that last week devoured a scuba diver, Luciano Costanzo, aged forty-seven.

The shark was seen by two people as it attacked its victim. They both identified it as a white shark, of the same family as the star of the film *Jaws*. Signor Costanzo was diving to examine undersea electricity cables in the Bay of Baratti, near Piombino. On a small motor-launch was his son, Luca, and Signor Paolo Bader, a friend. They say the shark attacked several times and then dragged its victim underwater. A search later found only small pieces of the body and torn fragments of his wet suit.

The actual hunt is without spectacular heroics. A police launch is searching with an underwater television camera, but it has a range of a couple of yards only.

Yesterday a shark cage was finally obtained and frogmen of the fire brigade are being slowly towed around in it. They also hope to find further remains of Signor Costanzo. His friends and colleagues have been trying to search for the shark themselves by diving normally, but have been stopped by the police.

Signor Carlo Gasparri, an expert diver who was once world spearfishing champion, is using a giant "mousetrap" baited with a dead sheep and claims that, if the shark is still around, it will not escape. He is also using huge steel fish-hooks with live fish as bait on a vertical line chained to anchored buoys.

As the hunt continues, the waterfront of the sleepy village of Baratti is becoming crowded with visitors. At the weekend small groups and families came with sandwiches and binoculars as the weather became unseasonably warm. There was not a single scuba diver to be seen.

The Times, London, 6 February 1989

Some of the anchored, baited hooks placed in the sea to catch the twenty-foot great white shark being hunted off the Tuscany coast have been torn from their moorings, it was discovered yesterday. In the hunt for the shark that killed a scuba diver last week, police divers have found the victim's air-tanks, his face mask and his ballast belt. The lead weights on his belt showed clearly the shark's teeth marks.

A number of residents along the coast between Piombino and San Vicenzo have claimed sightings

of the man-eater before and since the attack.
                    The Times, London, 7 February 1989

The hunt for the man-eating great white shark off
the coast of Tuscany has developed into a confused
free-for-all involving the Italian Coast Guard, the
Carabinieri, the fire brigade, a number of helicopters and amateur "avengers" who want to dive with
anti-shark guns.

The normally placid waters of the Gulf of Baratti
are being chopped up by hovering helicopters and
cruising launches. The search for the remains of Luciano Costanzo was officially called off two days ago
after recovering only some of the victim's equipment
and a few small fragments of flesh. But the search
for his killer, said to be twenty-five feet long, has
begun in earnest. Until yesterday only baited hooks
and a kind of giant steel mousetrap, using a dead
sheep as bait, had been used so as not to obstruct
the search for remains.

The official co-ordinator of the hunt is Signor
Carlo Gasparri, an expert diver. "There is no need
for helicopters," he said. "Sharks are hunted with
baited hooks and that's all. The rest is all nonsense."

Clearly, however, several would-be shark killers
do not agree and, as they hunt their quarry, curious
onlookers can be seen all around the bay, keeping
watch with binoculars, cameras and sandwiches.
The authorities receive several reports of sightings
every day from different points on the coast.

It seems the whole of Italy has suddenly become
shark mad. Most newspapers have reporters per-
manently on the spot and print interviews with
shark experts around the world. Each television

news bulletin has the latest report on the situation, and it is not unusual to hear housewives, barmen, barbers and taxi drivers giving impromptu conferences on the migratory and feeding habits of Carcharodon carcharias, the lethal great white.

Off the Tunisian coast fishermen reportedly caught a twenty-one-foot thresher shark on Saturday. The species has not been seen there for thirteen years. The fishermen cut open their prize to see if it might have been the wanted fish, but found no such evidence.

The only people not enthralled by the great shark hunt are the inhabitants of resort villages around Piombino. They fear the affair is being overplayed and will ruin the tourist trade this summer.

The Times, London, 8 February 1989

TASMANIA, AUSTRALIA, 1993

Theresa Cartwright cannot have known what hit her. The keen diver and mother of five children, including quadruplets, died instantly when she was torn in half by a fifteen-foot great white shark off the coast of Tasmania on the weekend.

Terri's husband, Ian, and the couple's children watched in horror from a boat, unable to help, as she was brutally savaged. The family saw the sea turn red after the two-ton creature snatched her. Mrs. Cartwright, 34, was last seen clamped in the shark's jaws. Part of her leg and a piece of wetsuit were found.

"The shark went at her like a train—she didn't stand a chance," said her husband, who was on a boat with the six-year-old quads—three boys and a girl—and the family's eleven-month-old baby.

The tragedy happened as Mrs. Cartwright, who became a national celebrity when she had the quads, was studying seals at Tenth Island, a rocky outcrop off northern Tasmania. She dived in with two friends, who reached the sea bed without problems, but she appeared to have difficulty with her air supply and was slower to descend. Police said sharks and killer whales were known in the area and Mrs. Cartwright was aware of the dangers.

Relatives of Mrs. Cartwright, who was from Kent, England, said yesterday they were in shock after hearing of the attack . . . Mrs. Cartwright and her husband emigrated to Australia in 1986. Bettine Cartwright, her mother-in-law, from Canterbury, said: "They were a wonderful couple, and I can't believe Terri has gone. It's just too terrible to think about."

London Daily Mail, 7 June 1993

CHATHAM ISLANDS, NEW ZEALAND, 1995

Diver Kina Scollay fought his way out of the jaws of death by beating off a sixteen-foot white shark with a rock. The twenty-two-year-old was close to being bitten in two by the huge predator, which clamped its jaws around his middle as he was gathering shellfish.

Horrified friends in nearby boats saw the giant shark burst to the surface with Mr. Scollay in its mouth. He was thrashing at it and screaming, "Don't let it get me, don't let it get me!" Seconds later the man-eater released its grip and Mr. Scollay was hauled from the water off the Chatham Islands, east of New Zealand.

"The shark was coming round to have another go at him, so we pulled him straight into the dinghy," said fisherman Richard Ennor. "As we pulled Kina up, the shark went under the dinghy. It was the scariest moment of my life."

Mr. Scollay's lead diving belt was mangled by the shark's teeth and his wetsuit was shredded. But he escaped with deep gashes in his legs and chest.

From his hospital bed in Christchurch, where he was air-lifted after the attack, Mr. Scollay described his ordeal. He said last night: "There were a few seconds of disbelief. I felt a pretty big grip across my waist and thought 'What the hell?' Then I looked down and there was this bloody great thing. That's when I realised it was a shark. There was initial panic and I tried to kick to the surface, but, because it had me by the legs, I started hitting it with a rock I'd been bringing back to the surface to show my friends.

"It was dragging me down, but it didn't take long for it to let me go. I was thinking more about getting away from it than being scared. Now I'm just so relieved that I've still got everything—my legs and all the other important bits. And I'm pleased to be here in hospital rather than lying on a slab."

Brave Mr. Scollay will not be able to dive again for at least two months, but he says the attack will not put him off, insisting, "You'd have to be pretty unlucky for it to happen twice."

London Daily Star, 1 December 1995

ISLE OF WIGHT, UNITED KINGDOM, 1995

A recent article in *Diver* magazine reported a shark sighting in the English Channel six miles off the Isle of Wight. The report states that a wreck diver, George Hayward, of RAF Odiham BSAC was diving with his buddy Trevor Jones on the wreck of the SS *Westville* in forty metres of water.

Descending the line head first Mr. Hayward received quite a shock when, at around the twenty-metre mark, "This shark of about two metres brushed against my mask as it went by, I was startled as it passed right against my nose!"

The men continued their dive despite this unexpected encounter. Mr. Jones said, "The funniest thing was that, when George first saw the shark, he clung on to the shot line and pulled his arms and legs in very tight. The wrecks out there are covered with pollack and mackerel, and that attracts sharks. We reckon it was a porbeagle."

A shark encounter underwater in the UK is a rare occurrence. Among the large sharks which can be found in UK waters are blues, makos, porbeagles, threshers, basking sharks and occasionally hammerheads. This summer [1995] has been the warmest since records began, leading to many sightings of unusual visitors to these waters including loggerhead turtles and sun fish.

Reuters, September 1995

FLORIDA KEYS, USA, 1995

A marine biologist from Livonia was killed during a shark attack while scuba diving for exotic fish off the Florida Keys, police determined on Thursday. William Covert, 25, was killed by a bull shark, said the Monroe County (Fla.) Sheriff's Department after reviewing the findings by marine biologists and shark experts.

"I don't think he ever saw the shark coming," said Covert's sister, Teresa Simonds of Garden City. "He was an experienced diver who had been to Brazil and around the world diving."

Covert had been missing since 13 September, when he disappeared while diving with friends for tropical fish off Alligator Reef, near Islamorada. His mother, Maryann Fiordelis, had been working with local dive teams in Key West and the Sheriff's Department to find her son.

"We kept thinking they would find him or that a boat had picked him up," Simonds said. "Today we finally realised that he wasn't coming home."

Thomas Scaturro, a Florida boat owner and exotic fish dealer, was with Covert on his boat the night he disappeared. Scaturro said Covert was the only diver using air tanks instead of thirty-foot compressed air hoses attached to the boat. "After about an hour of diving, I saw his tanks and equipment on the bottom of the ocean," Scaturro said.

The Coast Guard searched for two days, but found nothing. Because of rough weather, it took Scaturro and other dive teams a week to find and recover Covert's equipment and shreds of his dive clothing. Scaturro said the tanks found still had air in them, which led him to believe that Covert had not drowned.

Gordon Hubbell, a shark specialist in Key Biscayne, was one of several scientists who examined Covert's clothing and equipment, and determined he was killed by a bull shark. "I was able to match the bite marks on the dive belt and tee-shirt to a ten- to twelve-foot bull shark. The attack was quick and extremely vicious." Hubbell said the attack was very rare and noted that it was the first fatal shark attack of the year in Florida.

Covert was a graduate of Stevenson High School in Livonia and received his bachelor's degree in marine biology from Michigan State University in 1993.

Mrs. Fiordelis is expected to ask a Florida judge today to declare her son officially dead, said Covert's sister. "We just want this to be over. We don't want to wait seven years to have a funeral."

Detroit News, 22 September 1995

MIAMI, FLORIDA, USA, 1995

Florida is in the midst of a record year, a record the state would rather not have. So far this year, there have been twenty-five shark attacks in Florida waters. Experts believe there is a logical explanation for the increased number of incidents.

All summer long waves pounded Florida's east coast, driven in by one hurricane after another cruising north along the Atlantic seaboard. The larger waves have attracted more surfers and that, in turn, has led to more encounters with sharks. One surfer had his feet bitten by a shark.

CNN, 25 September 1995

CALIFORNIA, USA, 1995

The following report is an account of a shark attack on myself, Marco Flagg. It details the sequence of events to the best of my knowledge and experience . . .

Location of incident: outside Bluefish Cove, St. Lobos State Park, Monterey, California . . . Time of incident: approximately 5:30 pm on 30 June 1995. Weather: flat calm, minimal wind, no swell, reduced ambient surface light due to low clouds and relatively late time of day . . . About myself: I am a thirty-one-year-old diver, certified in 1988. I hold both a PADI Advanced Open Water and a NOAA working diver certification . . . By profession I am an electronics engineer . . .

I had been invited to some pleasure diving at Pt. Lobos by two friends, Steve and Marcie. We intended to make use of the good diving conditions which had lately been reported. After some engine trouble with the Zodiac inflatable early in the day, we finally started our first dive at about 2:55 pm. The dive lasted about forty minutes and my maximum depth was ninety-eight feet. The visibility was about ten feet at the surface and improving to about thirty feet at the bottom. After the first dive we left our dive site marker buoy in place and headed for shore for a late lunch and a surface interval.

At about 5:20 pm we started the second dive of the day. I was trying out Steve's diver propulsion vehicle (scooter) and, propelled by it, was descending through the water at an angle of about twenty degrees. After maybe two minutes and at a depth of about fifty feet, I looked to my right and saw the massive pectoral fin attached to the end of the torpedo shape of a large fish, which was about twenty feet away, at the edge of the range of visibility. Two or three seconds later the animal disappeared from view in the cloudy water.

Somewhat stunned, I at once thought the animal matched the shape and size of a great white shark—I had never seen one before live, but had seen plenty of footage recorded by other divers. While thinking that the shark was most likely just passing and would not attack me, I decided it would be prudent to return to the boat to warn Steve and Marcie, so I turned the scooter round and headed back towards the Zodiac. My ascent was at a gentle angle both because I did not want to suffer an air embolism by surfacing too fast and because, recalling that many shark attacks occur on the surface, I did not want to surface too far from the boat.

I was in an alert, apprehensive state, but still calm enough to think, with my peculiar sense of humour, "Gee, I got to see it without paying for a shark diving trip." At that moment I looked below to my left and saw the massive, wide open, nearly circular, teeth-lined mouth of the shark coming at me. The mouth appeared to have a diameter of between two and three feet.

"Oh, shit," I thought, and at once felt a severe but dull pressure on my body. I do not recall being shaken by the shark nor taking any significant evasive or defensive action. But after a few seconds I appeared to be free of its hold and I thought, "It didn't bite very hard." I tried to feel if my legs were still there, and they seemed to be, so, at maximum speed, I resumed my set course, attempting not to surface too rapidly close to the boat and not thrashing around in case this encouraged the shark to bite again.

Surfacing about twenty yards from the boat, I proceeded the rest of the way on the surface. Having reached the Zodiac . . . I climbed in and started to rev the engine in neutral in short bursts so as to warn Steve and Marcie. I had a dull pain in my gut, but reckoned there was probably no big loss of blood as I was still conscious. Steve surfaced after about three to five minutes . . . [and] Marcie several minutes later.

We left the marker buoy in place and headed to shore. I climbed out of the Zodiac on my own, but then sat down because I felt weak. The ambulance arrived within a few minutes . . .

I sustained a wound of about 1.75 inches in diameter on my left forearm (six stitches) with another one-inch scrape mark. A further eight stitches were required for a cut wound on my left upper leg.

The third cut wound is on my left lower abdomen, with a bruise in the vicinity. The distance from the leg wound to the arm wound is twenty inches if my arm is down and thirty inches if my arm is held up at an angle of forty-five degrees. I do not specifically recall what position my arm was in when the shark bit, but the fact that I was using the scooter suggests it should have been up . . .

My injuries from the incident are surprisingly light, considering the circumstances. One reason for this may be that the shark, for whatever reason, simply decided not to exert much force on my body. Another possibility is that, in fact, I got sandwiched between two layers of metal: the shark may have bitten on to the tank on my back and the dive tracker instrument on my front. The dive tracker instrument may well have been resting on my abdomen—its natural position. Thus, the pressure on the tank and on the dive tracker spread the force of the shark's bite over a large area and resulting in the bruise on my abdomen. If this is the case, my cut wounds may simply have been points where my body was "bulging out" between the instrument and the tank; in effect I was protected by a "sandwich" of armour . . .

Marco Flagg, Internet, 2 July 1995

CALIFORNIA, USA, 1994

A shark, apparently a great white, killed a commercial diver in the water off San Miguel Island on Friday—the state's first confirmed death from a shark attack in nearly six years.

Santa Barbara resident James Robinson, 42, was treading water near his boat when the shark swooped in for a swift, brutal attack. He had just finished a routine dive to scout for sea urchins and had deposited his equipment aboard his boat. His two crew members were putting away the equipment when they heard Robinson scream—and whirled around to see him drifting unconscious in a gush of blood.

"His right leg was nearly severed and his left leg had puncture wounds on it," said Francis Oliver, a diver who came to Robinson's aid after hearing his crewmates' distress call. "It was pretty gruesome."

A veteran diver, Robinson was attacked at about 9:45 am, half a mile off the coast of San Miguel Island, which lies about forty miles west of Santa Barbara. Crew members on Robinson's boat, the *Florentia Marie*, tried to revive him, but could not find a pulse. A Coast Guard helicopter rushed Robinson to Goleta Valley Community Hospital, where he was pronounced dead of massive trauma at 11:15 am.

Neither of the crew members saw the attack, but Coast Guard officials said they believe Robinson was targeted by a great white shark, a keen-eyed predator that can grow up to twenty feet in length and can sink its serrated teeth through a surfer and surfboard with one swift bite. "They say it's like a bullet—you never see the one that bit you," urchin diver Jeffery Gunning said. "I just hope it went quick for Jimmy."

Before entering the sea urchin business, Robinson

had worked for years as a deep-sea diver for an off-shore oil rig in the North Sea, near the English Channel. After settling in Santa Barbara, he quickly absorbed the California lifestyle. Deeply tanned with blond curly hair and an athletic build, Robinson loved surfing and diving—any activities which would keep him in the sun or in the water. Gracious and vivacious, Robinson was popular both in the harbour and in the neighbourhood. "You always hear about the good dying young and, golly, this guy was just one of the best," long-time diver Steve Rebuck said. "He will really be missed."

Most professional divers realize that great white sharks haunt the waters around San Miguel Island, where they feast on seals and sea lions, but their lurking presence has not deterred divers from prowling the ocean floor for valuable sea urchins, abalone and lobsters. It is a threat most divers take in their stride. "If you're frightened by it, you have no business being in the business," Rebuck said. "More people are killed by lightning and bee stings than by shark attacks."

Although great white sharks bump, bite and scare several people a year in California, fatalities are rare. No deadly attacks have been confirmed since UCLA graduate student Tamara McCallister was killed by a great white off Malibu in February 1989 (see p. 104) . . . In a more recent incident, a woman's shark-bitten body was found off the San Diego coast last April (see p. 147), but the county coroner said the victim may already have been dead when the great white gnawed at her body.

To protect themselves from attack, veteran divers usually descend to the ocean floor as quickly as possible. Once on the bottom, they can hide among rocks and shadows. Eventually, however, they must rise to the surface, where their wet-suited bodies are vulnerable. "It's one of the risks of diving," Gunning said. "We become part of the food chain when we enter the water." As a precaution, several divers in northern California have begun to tuck plastic pistols in their wet suits before jumping into shark-infested waters, Rebuck said. But most locals rely on more low-tech survival techniques—when face to face with a great white, they "say three Hail Marys and four Our Fathers," diver Matt Barnes said.

In the waters around San Miguel Island divers have learned to check for sharks by studying the behaviour of the sea lions and seals which carpet the beaches. If the animals look spooked or if any appear mauled, the divers know to stay away. Even the best precautions, however, are not fail safe. Sharks sometimes attack humans out of pure curiosity, marine biologist Gary Davis said, and they sometimes confuse divers in wet suits for sleek seals.

"They spend a lot of time bumping things on the surface and seeing if anything falls off," Davis said. "If it does, they taste it to see if it's something good to eat."

Divers are willing to face such risks in part because the sea urchin business can be quite lucrative. Sea urchin roe is a delicacy in Japan, prized for its rarity, freshness and delicate taste.

Los Angeles Times, 10 December 1994

CALIFORNIA, USA, 1993

A large great white shark attacked an abalone diver off the Mendocino County coast yesterday, half swallowing the man head first before spitting the struggling swimmer out.

David R. Miles, 38, of Eureka was hit as he and three friends were free snorkeling in thirty feet of water near the tiny coastal village of Westport, about four miles north of Fort Bragg.

"It swallowed him head first," a Coast Guard spokesman said in describing the near fatal encounter. "It happened so fast, he never knew what hit him." There was no estimate of the shark's size, but the spokesman added that any shark capable of half swallowing a man has to be considered large.

According to a spokesman at Mendocino Coast Hospital in Fort Bragg, Miles is in fair condition with bite wounds on his face, chest and back. He will be kept in the hospital overnight for observation.

The shark attacked shortly before 3 pm and either spit the diver out or loosened its bite enough for Miles to wriggle free. Miles then swam about thirty yards to the safety of rocks, where he was aided by his friends. A Coast Guard helicopter was used to lift Miles up a 200-foot bluff, where he was transferred to an ambulance and taken to the hospital.

Shark attacks are rare along that part of the north coast, according to Coast Guard officials. Most attacks have been further south. In Westport most of its one hundred or so residents were surprised by news of the shark attack. "We live off this ocean," said Marie Fostiak, who works at the Westport Community Store. "This whole town is talking about our shark. Not much else is getting done."

San Francisco Chronicle, 13 August 1993

BYRON BAY, AUSTRALIA, 1993

A newly-wed woman saw a great white shark kill her husband, 31, as he went diving at the Australian beauty spot of Byron Bay. A fishing boat later netted the sixteen-foot fish, which rammed it several times and dragged it nearly four miles out to sea before disgorging human remains and breaking free.

John Ford was grabbed by the shark as he was scuba diving. His wife, Deborah, who was also diving from their charter boat, was uninjured, but in shock after witnessing the attack from below the surface.

The attack came only five days after another 11.5-foot great white shark, known as "white pointers" in Australia, killed a thirty-five-year-old mother of quadruplets [Teresa Cartwright, see p. 42] who had been on a diving excursion near a seal colony off the southern island state of Tasmania.

The Times, London, 10 June 1993

GYOGO ISLAND, JAPAN, 1992

With one bite a shark wiped out this summer's tourist trade on the little Japanese island of Gyogo.

It attacked as Kazuta Harada was gathering shellfish on the ocean floor in his old-fashioned helmeted diving suit. He shouted, "Shark! Pull me up, pull me up!" but, by the time his crew could reel in the air line and intercom connection, there was nothing left. Just the gashed remains of his suit hung on the steel helmet.

Nobody saw the shark during the attack, although it had earlier bumped at the helmet of another diver, who feigned dead. Nobody saw it clearly after the attack either. One grainy photograph of a dorsal fin was the only firm evidence of its existence, but the fear was enough to destroy Gyogo's summer beach holiday business.

The people of Gyogo normally play host to thousands of visitors, who cross from the larger island of Shikoku and from the major cities hundreds of miles away to the north-east. This year nobody is coming, except a few morbid spectators hoping to be in on another kill. According to Japanese experts, the Gyogo attacker was probably a type of blue shark, a species which is found quite frequently off Britain's south-west coasts in September and October. It has never been known to kill anyone in British waters, although it has occasionally attacked boats, and the bad-tempered blue is certainly a confirmed man-eater elsewhere in its wide range.

The Times, London, 24 October 1992

ADELAIDE, AUSTRALIA, 1963

A twenty-three-year-old spear fisherman was badly mauled by a man-eating shark while competing in the State spear fishing championships at Aldinga Beach yesterday afternoon. The attack was the third—one fatal—in South Australia in less than three years.

Surgeons at the Royal Adelaide Hospital battled for four hours yesterday afternoon in a dramatic attempt to save the man's life after a high-speed dash by car and ambulance from Aldinga Beach.

The injured man is Mr. Rodney Fox, married, of Hammersmith Avenue, Edwardstown. He suffered severe chest injuries, a punctured lung, loss of blood, shock and badly gashed right hand. His condition last night was described as satisfactory.

The attack occurred at 12:45 pm in about fifteen feet of water about 200 yards north of the reef at Snapper Point, Aldinga Beach. It was within a few hundred yards of the point where spear fisherman Mr. Brian Rodgers of Woodville was badly mauled by a shark in March 1961. Mr. Fox was wearing a full-length black rubber suit with yellow stripes down the sides of the jacket, and blue flippers. The attack came suddenly, a few minutes after Mr. Fox had unloaded his catch of fish into a patrol boat.

Spear fishermen said they had not seen any sharks in the area during the day.

"Rodney was swimming about twenty yards from my boat when it happened," skipper Mr. J. B. Francis said afterwards. "Suddenly I saw him flipped over on his back. His goggles and snorkel came off, and blood started to colour the water. I didn't see the actual attack though."

Mr. Francis said he raced his fourteen-foot fibreglass boat, which is powered by a forty-five horse power outboard motor, towards the scene. With him in the boat was Mr. Brian Brawley from Henley.

"We had Rodney on board within a minute of the attack," Mr. Francis said. "We picked up another competitor, Mr. Bob Davis of Payneham, and raced for the reef. Brian and Bob assisted Rodney. They tried to hold him in a position so that he was leaning forward to keep the wounds closed. Rodney was bleeding badly from gaping wounds in his left side."

In the attack the shark drove its teeth through the left side of the thick rubber suit, ripping it from just above the armpit to the waist. The semi-circular imprint of the shark's teeth on the suit showed the size of its jaws. The shark is believed to have been a bronze whaler because spear fishermen said Mr. Fox had gasped, "It was a bronzie."

The chairman of the South Australian Council of Underwater Activities, Mr. J. Alexander, drove his car from the beach on to the reef to get as close to the boat as possible. "We didn't see anything from the beach. All we heard was someone shout, 'Shark attack.'" Mr. Alexander then set out immediately for Adelaide. Four miles south of Noarlunga on the Yankalilla road he met the ambulance, which reached the hospital within an hour of receiving the call.

One of the team of surgeons who operated on Mr. Fox said: "He's a very lucky lad, all things considered. His whole chest wall was badly shattered, the ribs crunched and part of the left lung punctured by the shark's teeth." The victim's right hand was considerably mauled—"It looked as though he'd tried to fend off the shark with his hand." At least two tendons had been seriously damaged and there was the further possibility of some damage to nerves. "But it looks as though he will not only keep his hand, but all of his fingers."

Mr. Fox has been spear-fishing for about six years and is a member of the King Neptune Spearfishing Club. He won the South Australian championship last year and was placed third in yesterday's championship, which was halted after the attack. Three boats were patrolling the sea in the vicinity of the competition.

After the attack competitors were cleared from the area. Previous victim Mr. Brian Rodgers said last night that the injuries to Mr. Fox's right hand indicated he had indeed attempted to ward off the shark. He had experienced the same set of circumstances when he was attacked. Mr. Rodgers said he was sitting on the reef at the time of yesterday's attack. He had got out of the water because he had had "a funny feeling": "I don't know whether it was a premonition or not, but there was quite a lot of blood in the water from speared fish."

The history of shark attacks in South Australian waters has followed a haphazard pattern. The first known fatal attack was in March 1926, when Mrs.

Primrose White died a few minutes after having been mauled at Brighton. Another person disappeared at West Beach in January 1936 after a shark had been seen to leap out of the water.

Adelaide Advertiser, 9 December 1963

ADELAIDE, AUSTRALIA, 1991

An experienced diver told yesterday how he heard a "thunderous roar" when his diving partner was taken by a shark off Aldinga Beach. Off-duty police officer Mr. Dave Roberts watched in horror underwater as the shark he estimated was four metres in length careered past him thrashing its head about.

"I could not see him, but I knew the shark had my buddy," Mr. Roberts said. "The thunderous noise was so loud I couldn't hear anything else."

A police spokesman said the dead man "had no warning. He was literally taken in one big grab."

The dead man, 19, of One Tree Hill, was a student at the University of Adelaide and was the ninth person to die in a shark attack in South Australian waters. Police have not released his name.

The shark, which Mr. Roberts believes was a white pointer [great white], took the young diver about 350 metres off Snapper Point, the main lookout at Aldinga Beach, at about 3 pm yesterday. The man was diving with a group of other students and members of the Adelaide University Skindiving Club in eighteen metres of water at a popular skindiving spot called the Drop Off. Three other people, including Mr. Roberts, were in the water in the vicinity of the tragedy, but no one else was attacked. Four others who had been part of the diving group had climbed aboard their boat minutes earlier.

By nightfall yesterday police had recovered the dead man's air tank, his diving finds and a small part of his body. The search was called off at dark, but will resume at first light today. The tank's rubber hose, which led to the mouthpiece, was severed.

Mr. Roberts, a senior constable in the police prosecuting branch, said the group was on its second dive of the day and he and his "buddy" (a diving term for partner) were returning to their boat when the shark struck.

"We were heading back to the boat, which was not far ahead of us, when I looked back at him and everything was all right," Mr. Roberts recalled. "I turned back and went down to have a look at this colourful rock, and then suddenly heard this thunderous noise. I turned again and saw the shark. It was close to me and it was thrashing its head around. The noise was very loud. It was like a boat crashing over waves on top of you. The whole bottom was dusted up. The shark kept thrashing from side to side. I couldn't make him out clearly, but I knew he was there. I hung around and took a defensive position behind the rock and it moved away. It came within one and a half feet of me as it went past. It didn't look at me. It just took my buddy first—just dragged him past me as I was behind the rock. It was totally unexpected—you just never see them out there. I don't know if I'll dive again—this scared the life out of me." .

Yesterday's dive had lasted about twenty minutes before the attack and had followed fourteen other dives by about thirty club members who were spending the day at Aldinga Beach. Ben Petersen, 18, of Aldgate, was first back to the boat and had helped three others into it when he suddenly heard screaming. "It was Dave Roberts screaming out 'Shark,' so I pulled the anchor up and we drove the boat over to him," Mr. Petersen said. "A tank, fins and other diving equipment floated by. We got Dave into the boat and he was saying a four-metre shark had come up and grabbed his mate."

Veteran Mr. Rodney Fox recalled last night how he was attacked in the same place in 1963: "It's an interesting place to dive—lots of fish gather there near a big drop off the reef." Mr. Fox had been defending his title as S. A. spear fishing champion when a white pointer hurled him through the water. He escaped after gouging its eyes and snout. Once he reached the surface he realised his chest was badly mutilated. Although he needed eighty-seven stitches, Mr. Fox became fascinated with white pointers and continues to research them. Mr. Fox continued with his sport and became involved in the making of several shark-attack movies, including *Jaws*, the Emmy-award-winning *Mysteries of the Sea*, and the South Australian Film Corporation's *Caged in Fear* television special. He is also a consultant to the Cousteau Society.

Adelaide Advertiser, 9 September 1991

CALIFORNIA, USA, 1990

An abalone diver was recovering at home yesterday in Santa Rosa, wounded but undaunted after he was attacked by an immense shark in waters off Jenner.

Rodney Orr, 49, was attacked at about 1 pm on Saturday by what appeared to be a great white shark as he was diving near some isolated rocks at Russian Gulch Beach. Orr, an electrician and part-time commercial fisherman, said yesterday that he was sitting on a paddle board about twenty-five yards off shore when the shark rammed into the board and knocked him into the water.

Seconds later, Orr said, the shark had his head and neck in its jaws. "My head was in its mouth—I could see the teeth at an angle."

At that instant, recalled Orr, his response was guided by the primitive instinct for self-preservation: he clobbered it with his spear gun. "I resorted to being a cave man and clubbed it. I was beating on him something fierce. I wasn't going to take this sitting down."

The shark let go and Orr got on to his board and paddled twenty minutes back to shore. His only wounds were gashes to his face and neck.

"It was a really frightening experience," he said. "You think you know what is going to happen to you, but then you really don't."

He was flown from the beach by helicopter to Community Hospital in Santa Rosa, where he was treated for moderate cuts to his nose, cheek and neck. Orr speculated that his injuries could have been more serious if he had not been wearing his diving hood, which now has holes in it. He has been a fisherman for more than twenty years and said it was his second encounter with a shark: he barely escaped a similar attack in the 1960s.

San Francisco Chronicle, 10 September 1990

CALIFORNIA, USA, 1990

On a quiet day at the Farallon Islands a great white shark tried to eat scuba diver LeRoy French of Concord. "I could feel his mouth around my body and then he chomped me," French said. "When his teeth bit into my metal air tank, he let me go."

Last fall, also at the Farallons, a giant shark grabbed diver Mark Tiserand of San Francisco by the leg and dragged him off, as if looking for a quiet spot for a meal. "He was swimming off with me so fast I could feel the water rushing past," Tiserand recalled.

Last week, twenty-five yards off the beach near Jenner, Rodney Orr of Santa Rosa was knocked off his paddle board, then got a close look at some pearly whites. "My head was in its mouth, I could see the teeth."

Episodes like these are making the Bay Area coast the shark attack centre of the world. A search through this paper's files reveals there have been more than fifty shark incidents recorded off the Bay

Area alone, though most receive little attention in the media. French, Tiserand and Orr all survived by fighting off their attacker. French and Tiserand had their lives saved when they were airlifted by helicopters to hospitals for emergency surgery. French ended up with a scar that runs four feet down his side, Tiserand with shark teeth souvenirs that doctors removed from his leg. Orr just about had his head bitten off, but escaped with big gashes around his left eye and neck. The shark lost interest when Orr clubbed him with his spear gun.

Waters off the Bay Area coast have sharks of mind-boggling size. In one fifty-minute period at the Farallon Islands, scientist Peter Klimely of Scripps Institute chummed up and tagged three different great whites that were all seventeen feet long. A few years back, at Ano Nuevo State Reserve in San Mateo County, a shark measuring nineteen feet and weighing an estimated 5,000 lbs. washed up on the beach. That is as big as the one in the movie *Jaws*.

After a career of studying sharks, scientist John McCosker of the Steinhart Aquarium in San Francisco has identified the zone where the attacks are most common. "I call it the Red Triangle," said McCosker, who has travelled throughout the world to study man-eaters. The Triangle is bordered by Ano Nuevo to the south, the Farallon Islands twenty-five miles out to sea to the west and Tomales Bay to the north.

Both Ano Nuevo and the Farallons are breeding grounds for elephant seals, and the young 200-lb. pups make perfect meals for the big sharks. The mouth of Tomales Bay, meanwhile, is believed to be a breeding ground for great whites.

Anywhere near the Triangle, it may be foolish to spearfish, dive for abalone, surf, swim or kayak. Yet these sports remain popular because months can go by without an incident—and also because the history of danger is unpublicised. Yet the attacks just keep happening. In January a shark knocked surfer Sean Sullivan of Pacifica off his surfboard, leaving bite marks in the board. Sullivan reportedly escaped by getting back on his board and surfing into the beach with the shark chasing him.

I never gave the idea of a shark eating me any thought until a fall day about ten years ago. I had arrived at Pigeon Point lighthouse, where there are a few secluded coves nearby that are ideal for body surfing, but this time there was a crowd at the beach. It turned out that an abalone diver had just been bitten in half and killed at the exact spot I was planning to swim that day.

Since then there have been many other episodes. While fishing at the Farallon Islands with Abe Cuanang, the boat anchored, our depth finder was reading the bottom as 90 feet deep. Suddenly it was reading 65 feet, then 50 feet. It made no sense.

Then, all at once, it did make sense. "It's the Big Guy," Cuanang shouted. The Big Guy in this case was a great white so large under the boat that it was registering as the bottom of the ocean on the depth finder.

The same week Ski Ratto of Pacifica was fishing in his seventeen-foot Boston Whaler when he sensed "something was looking at me." Ratto looked behind him and a great white four feet across at the head, possibly longer than the boat, was on the surface, and it was indeed looking at him. "I started the engine and got the hell out of there."

Ever since these episodes I have not been one to dangle my legs over the side of the boat or body surf, abalone dive or anything else that means being in the water with the Big Guy. As long as other people do, it is inevitable that every once in a while someone will be attacked by a shark.

San Francisco Chronicle, 16 September 1990

CAPE PROVINCE, SOUTH AFRICA, 1990

A twenty-one-year-old Johannesburg woman died yesterday after being attacked by a shark while diving off Mossel Bay.

Miss Monique Price was diving with her fiancé, Mr. Francois Suanepoel, and a friend when attacked about 500 metres from the shore at 4 pm.

The three had intended to salvage an anchor from a boat and had been in the water only a few minutes when the shark attacked Miss Price about seventy metres from the boat.

She was rushed to hospital in Mossel Bay and died just before 6 pm. She is reported to have suffered severe lacerations of her upper left thigh and to have lost a large amount of blood.

The last shark attack at Mossel Bay was only nine months ago, when a Cape Town surfer was badly bitten.

Cape Times, 25 June 1990

WESTERN PROVINCE, SOUTH AFRICA, 1989

A Table View diver narrowly escaped death when he was attacked by a shark while spearfishing in Smitswinkel Bay near the Cape Point Nature Reserve yesterday. The diver, twenty-nine-year-old Gert van Niekerk, suffered wounds to his chest and abdomen when the shark—believed to be a great white—attacked him about 250 metres from the beach yesterday afternoon.

Speaking from his False Bay hospital bed last night, Mr. Van Niekerk said the force of the shark's attack ripped his diving goggles off his face. "I did not see the shark. The first thing I saw was the water turning brown."

He immediately started swimming to the beach, leaving his spear gun behind. On the beach bystanders applied emergency medical treatment and he was stabilised before being carried over a ridge to the road. "Four guys on the beach treated me and then carried me about 1.5 kilometres. They were very good," he said.

Mr. Van Niekerk said he had been diving for the past five years, but yesterday's attack was his first brush with a shark. He had dived at the same spot previously without seeing any sharks. "I'm just glad the shark did not come back."

The attack was the third on divers in False Bay in six years. In October 1987 a Matie student was savaged by an enormous shark near Seal Island while spear fishing, and in 1983 a Springbok spear fisherman, Mr. A. Louw, was attacked by a four-metre shark at the same spot. Both men survived the attacks.

Cape Times, 18 September 1989

CALIFORNIA, USA, 1989

Larry Stroup, a veteran diver on his first shark-filming expedition, was capturing what he hoped would be dramatic footage. The camera was rolling and a five-foot blue shark—a species not known for its aggressiveness—was banging its snout against the bubble-like lens. Moments later, Stroup was fighting for his life.

"I felt a tug on my arm, and I looked over and his mouth was around my arm," Stroup, 46, recalled on Monday, a day after surviving a rare shark attack off the Channel Islands about thirty-five miles off Santa Catalina Island. "He just wouldn't let go."

Stroup, an Albuquerque real estate developer, smiled cheerfully while recounting the harrowing incident at Harbor-UCLA Medical Center in Torrence, where he is recovering from emergency surgery late on Sunday after being bitten on both arms. Doctors said he may be hospitalised for a week and may suffer at least temporary loss of movement in his right arm, where the shark's teeth ripped through muscles and ligaments. But, as a happy Stroup was quick to point out, it could have been worse.

"Compared to the alternatives, it was a very good event," he quipped. "Right now I couldn't tell you if I will dive with sharks again."

From a wheelchair with an intravenous bottle hanging above him, a refreshed, pyjama-clad Stroup told reporters there was no obvious reason that the shark turned on him. The attack occurred late on Sunday morning about ten miles north-west of Santa Barbara Island. Stroup was one of several divers aboard the sixty-foot *Scuba Lover*, a vessel hired out of Ventura Marina for a three-day recreational cruise aimed at observing and photographing the blue shark near a popular diving spot known as Lost Reef.

Members of the expedition—including an experienced shark diver and a veteran marine biologist—conducted many of their observations from within a ten-foot shark cage, but they also ventured outside the protective cage on several occasions to get a better look at the sharks, Stroup said. The practice is routine when viewing blue sharks if there are few of them and they are behaving passively, he added.

On Sunday, during a dive only a few feet below the surface, two senior divers left the shark cage in waters occupied by eight or ten blue sharks, Stroup recalled. At their signal that it was safe, Stroup also emerged from the cage, leaving one other diver behind. Almost immediately, he said, a shark approached him, bumping its nose repeatedly against his video camera. The behaviour was not unusual, so the amateur film-maker kept on shooting his adventurous home movie.

"I had just gotten out of the cage about fifteen seconds earlier," Stroup recalled, "there was nothing to warn us. It was butting its head against my camera, so I can't really say it snuck up on me. What surprised me was when he reached out and grabbed my arm."

Stroup did not feel any pain at first, only a strong tug, he said, but the shark held tight to his right arm. With his camera and his left arm, Stroup tried desperately to free himself from the shark's jaws as blood billowed out of his wet suit.

"All I could see was its snout," the diver said of the shark. "I saw its teeth. They weren't that big, but they looked sharp."

Los Angeles Times, 5 September 1989

LOUISIANA, USA, 1989

Carl Loe did not have to turn around to know what had happened. Nothing but a shark could clamp down on his leg with that kind of force. He turned anyway and watched as the six-foot sand tiger chomped and chomped again, then twisted its grip as if trying to tear off his right leg.

"When I turned and looked, there was nothing but teeth embedded in my leg," Loe said.

Loe, who was spearfishing on Saturday forty miles off the coast of Cocodrie, Louisiana, suffered dozens of puncture wounds and lacerations on both legs, as well as muscle and tissue damage. The forty-five-year-old Slidell furniture retailer was rescued by helicopter and treated at Ochiner hospital. Doctors tell him he should make a full recovery, but they are watching out for infections. Survival did not seem so certain for a long fifteen seconds on Saturday on Loe's fourth dive of the morning.

Loe and his partner, Arthur Bukaskey, were more than one hundred feet under water near the floor of the Gulf of Mexico, swimming among the pipes of an oil rig. The pipes offered Loe and Bukaskey an edge in their battle with the swift and strong fish they were hunting. It was comforting to know, Loe said, that, if he speared a big barracuda or an angry amberjack, he could tether his line to one of the rig's pipes and win the tug-of-war with the fish.

Loe said they were not looking for sharks, but sometimes they hunt them as well. They had been under water less than a minute when Loe spotted a shark lurking in the murky water near the bottom. He swam away from it and let Bukaskey fire his custom-made fifty-six-inch spear. Bukaskey's shot was true, and the stunned shark fled. Bukaskey was pulled along for the ride. He did not panic, though. He knew the 150-lb shark would soon tire and he would tow it back to the surface. He got back safely with his prize.

Meanwhile, Loe turned and aimed at a small sheep's head. Seconds after he fired, he felt the clamp close on him. It was a second shark, one he never saw. Loe later theorized that the unseen attacker might have been responding to the distress signals of the speared shark.

He could feel the jaws opening and closing again, trying to get a better grip, mauling his right leg and poking a few stray teeth through his left leg. Using the butt of his speargun, he rammed the nose of the shark again and again.

"My only reaction was to punch him on the nose and get him off," Loe said. It worked. Loe, hoping the shark would not come back "for seconds," swam quickly to the surface, where his fifteen-year-old son, Carl Loe III, worked to stop the bleeding and called for help.

So on Monday, as he sat propped up in his hospital bed, his fishing cap on the nightstand, the life-threatening experience was already beginning to sound like a fisherman's story, with a touch of bravado. Loe stroked his bushy grey beard and considered his future in spear hunting.

"It's just a dangerous recreational sport," said Loe, who hunts most of the fish for food and kills an occasional shark for a trophy. "The statistics [of shark attacks] are so rare and so extreme that I don't think it's going to keep me from diving . . . I may be quite a bit more cautious from now on though."

New Orleans Times-Picayune, 20 June 1989

CALIFORNIA, USA, 1986

A twenty-seven-year-old scuba diver was critically injured on Saturday when he was attacked just off a beach near Carmel by what experts said was probably a great white shark.

Frank Gallo of San Jose suffered a punctured right lung and lacerations to his right shoulder, jaw, neck and forearm in the 10 am attack off Carmel River State Beach, a spokesman for Community

Hospital of the Monterey Peninsula said. Gallo underwent a four-hour operation by four surgeons beginning at noon.

"He's doing incredibly well considering what he went through," said Charles Bancroft, a ranger at Point Lobos State Park, who was on duty near the beach and went to the hospital later. "He's going to have quite a story to tell."

Bancroft said one of the doctors told him the size of the bite wounds made it likely a great white shark, at least twelve to fifteen feet long, was responsible. The ranger said he was aware of only two previous shark attacks in the last five years, both involving great whites.

The beach, known locally as Monastery Beach, was closed after the attack, said Claude Wilkerson, a park aide.

Bancroft said Gallo, a paramedic for the Morgan Hill Fire Department and a competition scuba diver, was diving with two friends and was about 150 yards off shore and thirty feet beneath the surface when the attack occurred. He came to the surface and waved that he was in trouble, then his friends carried him to shore on a diving mattress and called an ambulance, according to the park ranger.

"He was very alert and talking to medical people the whole time," said Bancroft. "He said he never saw the shark, but managed to brush it off and it didn't attack him again."

Los Angeles Times, 7 December 1986

SOUTH AUSTRALIA, AUSTRALIA, 1985

A massive hunt to track down and destroy a killer
shark is due to start in Port Lincoln today. Divers
in the area have described it as the biggest hunt of
its kind mounted in the State.

It follows the horrific attack on Sunday on Port
Lincoln housewife Shirley Ann Durdin, 33, who was
torn in two and devoured by a six-metre white
pointer [great white] shark.

A special meeting organised last night by the Port
Lincoln Skin Diving Club and attended by abalone
divers as well as members of the Port Lincoln Game
Fishing Club, decided on the hunt. At least five vessels, including one from Adelaide, will take part in
the hunt for the killer shark. The first boat is due to
begin the search at about 10:30 am. Others will join
later today.

Two large nine-metre search vessels will stay out
at sea off Wiseman's Beach, north of Port Lincoln,
where Mrs. Durdin was taken by the shark while
diving for scallops on Sunday afternoon with her
husband, Barry, and a friend. The others, smaller
six-metre abalone boats, will resume the search
each morning. The search vessels will fan out from
a series of centre points off the coast in the Port Lincoln area in a bid to lure the giant shark into a spe-
cific area.

Whale oil and tuna blood will be poured into the
sea from the search vessels to attract the shark. Spe-

cial shark hooks will be baited and attached to floating drums, which will act as "positive anchors" if the shark takes the bait. The bow on each vessel will be armed with shotguns and high-velocity weapons to kill the shark if it is hooked. The fishermen, who are concerned for the safety of abalone divers operating in the area, are prepared to spend several days searching for the white pointer . . .

Kevin Bruce Wiseman has lived almost half his life in a rudimentary tin shed in the idyllically set Peake Bay on the Eyre Peninsula. The fifty-eight-year-old retired fisherman has become such a familiar figure in the area that locals now refer to that stretch of white beach about thirty-five kilometres north of Port Lincoln as Wiseman's Beach. That was until Sunday, when the serenity of the picturesque bay was shattered by the shark attack which brought death in the afternoon to a mother of four young children.

Mrs. Durdin of Lipson Place, Port Lincoln, was snorkelling for scallops with her husband of fifteen years, Barry, and a family friend when the six-metre shark struck in two-metre deep water as her three daughters and son watched from the shore 150 metres away.

"It will never be the same again," mourned Mr. Wiseman. "I loved this place for its peace and quietness, but that's changed now, hasn't it? I've seen a helluva lot of sharks in my day, but I've never seen anything as big as that one. The awful thing was I could only stand there and watch and do absolutely nothing. And what is probably even worse is that that shark will be back again."

Veteran shark catcher Neville Osborn, 46, said:

"This one now has the taste of human flesh and he'll be back." Osborn and his friend Colin Wood, 52, were fishing near Wiseman's Beach on Sunday afternoon when the great shark passed within metres of their boat. It was only hours after the shark had torn Mrs. Durdin in two and devoured her. The two men are now planning to hunt the shark in what they believe is one of South Australia's few remaining long-line shark boats.

A specialist in diving medicine, Dr. Carl Edmonds, said the return of the shark to the area was likely. He said the attack had been made for food or to protect the shark's territory. "The likelihood of shark attacks depends on two things: how many people are in the water and how many sharks are in the water," he said. "It is a worry when something like a white pointer, which is an open-ocean shark, comes into sheltered waters. It is certainly a cause for concern." Dr. Edmonds added that sharks did not eat because they were hungry; they react to stimuli such as someone flapping around on the surface.

Mr. and Mrs. Durdin had only recently moved back to Port Lincoln after Mr. Durdin, 35, suffered a number of allergies associated with work on his farm at Karkoo. Mrs. Durdin had just completed a course in farm management at Port Lincoln's TAFE College. Her distraught mother-in-law said yesterday that Shirley had loved the water since childhood.

Mr. Rob Kretschmer, who watched the attack from the shore, said he had to help restrain Mr. Durdin from going back into the water after his wife. "The friends they had been snorkelling with had to hold him down on the rocks to stop him going back in. He was distraught and hysterical and kept saying over and over, 'My wife, she's gone, she's gone.' "

A police spokesman at Port Lincoln said that there were no immediate plans to issue a general warning to the public about the shark danger. Meanwhile, police combed the shoreline in search of remains of Mrs. Durdin, while a local Department of Fisheries vessel searched the waters. But all that has been found is a single flipper and police have yet to ascertain whether it belonged to Mrs. Durdin.

Adelaide Advertiser, 5 March 1985

WESTERN PROVINCE, SOUTH AFRICA, 1985

A Plumstead man is especially pleased to be helping at a neighbour's wedding today—he survived an attack by what he believes to have been a great white shark at Buffels Bay, near Cape Point, yesterday.

Mr. Donald James was bitten in the ribs, the shark's teeth piercing two wet-suits and puncturing his right side. He said that he felt as though someone had stood on his rib cage, but was obviously "pleased to be alive to tell the tale." He had been spearfishing with a friend, Mr. Tullio Testa, about midday yesterday.

"We hadn't caught anything, so that dispels the myth that sharks attack when attracted by catches of fish," he asserted. "I felt something grab me and thought for a moment it might be Tullio playing a trick on me. Then I turned round and saw the shark, my first, instantaneous thought was 'Dumb shark, what do you want me for?'

"It let go of me and swam away and circled around. I wasn't going to wait for it to come back, so I headed for the kelp, where I came up and called for Tullio. I saw that the shark had followed us to the kelp, which dispels the myth that sharks won't go into kelp."

Mr. James ascribed his escape to the fact that he was wearing two wet-suits. Although both were punctured, the outer diving jacket had prevented blood from pumping into the water. He said he had checked the bite pattern against a reference book and thought the shark to be a great white. "I saw its eye, which was round and black, and that matches the description of a great white's eye," he said. He estimated the shark to have been about four metres long.

Cape Times, 5 January 1985

CALIFORNIA, USA, 1982

When marine biologist Michael Herder felt a tug on his arm while diving for abalone, he thought he had become entangled in kelp. But the tug was from a great white shark. In a brief battle in fifteen feet of murky water 200 yards off the Mendocino County coast, Herder suffered wounds that required more than 100 stitches.

"I didn't have a whole lot of time to think," Herder,

28, said in a telephone interview from his home in McKinleyville. "About the time I realised there was any real fight, the shark had let me go."

Herder, who works for the state Department of Fish and Game, said he and two companions, Scott Sterner and Leo Millan, were diving in the chilly waters of Bear Harbor on 19 September.

The shark first seized Herder under his left armpit, leaving no marks on him, but puncturing his rubber wetsuit. Herder reached around and pushed at the shark's head. The great white, which he estimated at twelve to fourteen feet long and more than 800 lbs, then bit a second time, slashing into his buttocks and upper thigh with razor-sharp teeth.

"The shark released me then—let me go—and took off to the north," he said. "I headed back to the boat."

Herder says his wounds did not hurt for some time, probably because the cold water numbed him and stemmed the flow of blood. "When I got to shore was the first time I began to feel pain," he recalled. "I couldn't walk unassisted. It looks like I was real lucky. There are no nerves severed and no permanent muscle damage. I should regain full use of all my appendages. If the shark had bitten as hard on my upper body as he did on my butt, I would have been in serious trouble."

Herder's advice is never to dive when visibility is less than fifteen feet. "The visibility was so low, it might have mistaken me for a seal and let me go once it decided I wasn't what it wanted for lunch."

Los Angeles Times, 26 September 1982

FLORIDA, USA, 1981

A wounded, six-foot-long mako shark "out for revenge" attacked the nineteen-year-old snorkeler who shot him on Monday, but the youth escaped with a relatively mild bite on the leg. Ted Best, a student at an auto mechanics schools, was flown by helicopter to the Pensacola hospital, treated for "about a hundred" puncture wounds in his right leg and given a pair of crutches before he was released.

Best said he was snorkeling in twelve feet of water off the Gulf Island National Seashore Park when two sharks approached him while he was looking for shells about fifty yards off shore.

"They went off and I kept an eye on them," Best recalled. He said he surfaced for air and submerged again, and, "The next thing I knew—I guess it was a mako—he was right up on me. I hadn't provoked him. I hadn't shot a fish to make blood or anything. They've always minded their own business, but these two looked like they were out for revenge or something. They went by and then, before I knew it, he was right on me. I always carry a speargun and I shot him. I pulled the spear out of him, but, before I could get it back in the gun, he hit me. I was pretty scared because I knew what they can do to you. When he bit my leg, I didn't know how bad it was. I just remember looking at his eyes. He looked me in the eyes. I'll never forget that."

Best said the shark released his leg and moved

away. He struck out for shore. One of the sharks followed him for a while and he saw "a black form" behind him in about seven feet of water, but then it disappeared. He scrambled ashore, breaking his face mask on a piling in the process, reached his car and drove himself to the ranger's station about half a mile from the beach. He was then flown in a helicopter to the Pensacola hospital.

New Orleans Times-Picayune, 25 August 1981

FLORIDA, USA, 1980

As darkness neared, sharks began circling the two scuba divers separated from their boat and one of them told himself, "This is the beginning of the end."

"It has already started," Greg EuDaly, 33, thought when he felt the first shark nudge him. But EuDaly and his companion, Chuck Castonguay, 38, were rescued when a third diver, Richard Schau, who stayed in the boat, radioed the Coast Guard and a Navy helicopter lifted them from the water on Sunday night as they fought the sharks off with their divers' knives.

"We were spearfishing in about ninety feet of water twenty-three miles off Jacksonville," EuDaly said in an interview on Thursday. "At that depth you always leave a man in the boat. Richard was in the boat and there was a current. It was pushing the boat one way and myself and Castonguay on the bottom of the ocean the other way."

When the two divers came to the surface, Schau

was a mile away in the boat and could not see his companions. Trouble, thought EuDaly, we're in big trouble. "In the first few moments, I went into panic," he added. "I'd never been in this situation before." But EuDaly, a former Navy man, began to remember some of the things taught him in air-sea rescue.

He and Castonguay lashed themselves as best they could to their scuba flotation devices and empty air tanks. "The seas were getting rough and nasty," he said. "Eight-foot waves. We began rigging ourselves for a stay."

In the meantime Schau kept his position, radioed the Coast Guard and explained the situation. Within an hour a Navy helicopter had been dispatched from the Jacksonville Naval Air Station. The sharks, though, came before sundown. EuDaly said they liked him best.

"I was only wearing the top of a wet suit. Chuck was wearing a full wet suit. I had been in air-sea rescue in west Florida. I told Chuck about the night two guys over there were in the same trouble and they found them. I didn't tell him only one of them survived!"

EuDaly began striking at the sharks with his diving knife as they came close, adding, "I thought then our chances were nil, but I wasn't giving up."

Schau said he could hear the helicopter when it arrived, but the helicopter crew apparently could not see him. He found a flare and lit it. The helicopter then began searching the area for the divers. Castonguay had a small diving light and he waved it furiously. When the chopper moved toward them,

EuDaly said, "It was the best sight I ever saw in my life."

Castonguay went up in the horse-collar hoist first. EuDaly thought he was home free, but, "Dog gone, if I didn't feel something at my legs. I looked down. It was a shark again. There is this halo above me with all the noise and the lights, and the rotors' spray—and the shark is at me." He stabbed at the shark's head and finally was hoisted out of reach.

New Orleans Times-Picayune, 3 October 1980

CAROLINE ISLANDS, PACIFIC, 1973

"It is probably the most basic human fear: getting attacked by a wild animal. When a grey reef shark tore open my left hand, I remember feeling as if I had been hit by a sledgehammer. Such was the shock that I do not recall the actual bite."

The incident took place in 1973 in a remote Micronesian lagoon in the Caroline Islands. Underwater photographer and diver Bill Curtsinger was swimming alone, ascending in a slow spiral after a dive, when he noticed the shark.

"It was twenty feet away and closing. I saw it sweeping its head back and forth; its back was arched like a cat's. The shark was 'speaking' to me, but at the time I didn't know the 'words.' The shark came at me like a rocket. I had time only to lift my hand, the shark ripping it with its teeth. As I swam frantically toward the boat, I saw that each dip of my hand left a cloud of blood in the water.

"The shark struck again, raking my right shoulder. At that moment a friend in a dinghy rescued me.

"The next day I posed with my bandaged wounds. Later I had minor surgery on my hand and shoulder. I was lucky, yes, but this defensive animal, I realised later, was not trying to eat me. It was, in fact, driving me away, quite possibly seeing me as a potential predator.

"Since then I have learned defensive behaviour myself. When photographing in Bikini Atoll, I sometimes donned a stainless steel mesh suit and slipped into a plastic 'shark scooter.' "

National Geographic, January 1995

WESTERN AUSTRALIA, AUSTRALIA, 1967

A shark bit a spearfisherman in half near Jurien Bay, one hundred miles north of Perth, at the weekend.

Robert Bartle, aged twenty-three, of Princess Road, Doubleview, Perth, died instantly. He had gone to Jurien Bay with seven other Perth skindivers for a spearing competition. Mr. Bartle was swimming from the shore to a reef about 800 yards out to sea with another spearfisherman, Lee Warner, aged twenty-four, five times holder of the state spearfishing title, when he was attacked by the shark, believed to be a white pointer [great white].

Mr. Warner said last night: "The shark came out

of the blue like a rocket and grabbed him when we were about eight feet down. It moved so fast that by the time I looked back, it had Bob in its mouth and was shaking him like a leaf. I dived straight down. It was directly below me. I put a spear in the top of its head, but it had no effect. The shark broke Bob in half and rose up at me.

"I only had an empty five-foot gun and I tried to hit the shark in the eye. It began circling, keeping about eight feet away. Its body looked about five feet thick, and it was an enormous length.

"By now I was swimming in a cloud of blood. I realised I was helpless without a spear, so I got Bob's, which was only a few feet away below the surface. I tried to belt the spear into the shark's eye, but the spear went just over the top of his head. The shark continued circling and I could see its mouth was about two-and-a-half-feet wide. Its teeth stuck out past its nose.

"I was stuck in this big cloud of blood. I knew Bob was dead. A little bronze whaler shark came and began darting around. I swam backwards fast. The blood was obscuring my vision. After about ten yards I got out of the blood. From 150 yards I could look back and see the blood, and the shark moving around tangled in the lines and our fishing gear.

"I felt pretty helpless. I kept stopping and looking back, convincing myself the shark was back there. I was still frightened. When I got to the beach I ran for help. We later recovered what was left of Bob's body. The shark swam away into deep water."

The Australian, 21 August 1967

QUEENSLAND, AUSTRALIA, 1966

A skin diver had his shoulder mauled by a seven-foot shark while he swam in forty feet of water about eleven miles from Heron Island. The attack took place off Broomfield Island at about 5 pm on Monday.

The diver is Barry Davidson, married, of New South Wales. He was taking underwater photographs when he saw the shark coming fast at him. He prodded it off with his speargun and saw it move towards a reef. The moment he turned, the shark was on him, but he frightened it off and surfaced.

He was taken by launch to Gladstone yesterday and will probably be flown to Sydney for a skin graft operation. Davidson said the shark had a fishing hook and part of a line caught in its mouth.

Brisbane Courier Mail, 28 September 1966

VICTORIA, AUSTRALIA, 1964

A twenty-nine-year-old skindiver lost his left leg in a shark attack while playing with a school of seals off Lady Julia Percy Island, near Port Fairy, 180 miles west of Melbourne. The diver, Henri Bource, of East Hawthorn, Melbourne, was in a serious condition in Warrnambool Hospital late last night.

Shark Attacks

The attack occurred when Bource and two other Melbourne skindivers, Dietmar Kruppa, 24, of Fitzroy, and Fred Arndt, of St. Kilda, were playing with the seals in thirty feet of water about fifty yards from their boat. The shark, an eight-foot tiger, charged at Bource, who was unarmed, from underneath the seals.

Kruppa and Arndt answered his screams for help. They fought off the shark with their spears as it circled Bource several times before swimming away.

Kruppa, a German-born motor mechanic, said, "We were diving down to tickle the seals. Suddenly there was a swirl in the water and clouds of blood. I heard Henri scream. Then I saw his leg floating in the water. It was the most horrifying sight of my life."

Kruppa said the three divers, wearing rubber suits, flippers, masks and snorkels, were about fifty yards from the boat when the shark attacked.

"We were having a lot of fun playing with the seals," he said. "Fred was with Henri and I was about ten yards away. Fred and I had short hand spears, but Henri was unarmed. The shark must have shot out from a pack of seals and caught Henri by surprise. He didn't stand a chance. Henri is more interested in underwater photography and quite often he does not carry a spear.

"Henri screamed: 'Save me, save me,' and we swam to him. Fred had seen the shark with a flipper in its mouth, but thought it was a seal. There was blood everywhere in the water and then I saw the shark circling Henri and coming in to attack again. He was a big brute—about eight feet.

"Henri was so brave. He kept calm as the shark

circled again and again as Fred and I jabbed it away with our short spears. I don't think Henri was in great pain—he was too shocked—but he kept his head and yelled his blood group to the people in the boat." Kruppa said Bource had been petting a dog on the beach and in the boat, and the shark may have been attracted by its scent.

Mr. Wal Kelly, captain of the boat from which the men were diving, said he heard one of the men call out, "Help me, help me." When he reached the swimmers, Bource's girlfriend, Miss Jill Ratcliffe, of St. Kilda, wearing skindiving gear, took a rope and jumped in. When Bource was aboard, Mr. Kelly sent an urgent radio message appealing to anyone hearing it to get in touch with Port Fairy police. He requested that a doctor be at the wharf for a transfusion.

The boat returned to Port Fairy by about 4 pm. Two doctors were waiting and immediately gave the transfusion.

The *Roma Kay* was being used by members of the Victorian Aqualung Club and a local club for diving with several underwater cameras.

Bource, a real estate agent and saxophonist leader of a Melbourne rock-and-roll band, is regarded as one of Victoria's best aqualung divers. Mr. H. J. Bource said his son did not like spearfishing and had refused to enter the recent State aqualung championships. "He does not like killing fish. He would rather take underwater movies of them," he said.

Mr. Bource added that Jill told him Henri had tried to free his leg by thrusting his arm down the shark's throat. He then gouged the shark's eyes to loosen its grip. "Jill was very brave. She had to be held back because she wanted to go straight back into the water and spear the shark."

Sydney Morning Herald, 30 November 1964

SOUTH AUSTRALIA, AUSTRALIA, 1962

A sixteen-year-old spearfisherman was fatally mauled by a man-eating shark while competing in skindiving competitions near Normanville yesterday afternoon. It was the third fatality from shark attacks in South Australian waters in thirty-six years and it came twenty-one months after another spearfisherman had been badly mauled at Aldinga Beach.

In a gallant rescue bid a fellow spearfisherman tied the injured youth to his surf ski and beat the shark off for ten minutes with a paddle before making it to the shore.

The dead youth was Geoffrey Martin Corner, son of Mr. and Mrs. A. M. Corner, of Nautilus Road, Elizabeth East, who were on the beach at the time of the attack.

The attack, one of the most vicious ever known in South Australian waters, occurred about 150 yards off shore from the Carrickalinga Beach, locally known as "the Gold Coast," two miles north of Normanville. The boy was attacked by the shark in twenty feet of water at 2:30 pm while taking part in the Underwater Skin Divers and Fishermen's Association in South Australia competitions.

The shark circled several of about sixteen other spearfishermen within 200 yards of Mr. Corner before lunging at him as he made his dive. The shark, believed to be a fourteen-foot bronze whaler, grabbed the boy's right leg between the calf and the thigh in its two-foot jaws and shook him violently before releasing him.

The attack was seen by fellow club member Allen Phillips, 27, of Reedle Street, Henley Beach, who was about ten yards away, towing a surf ski. Mr. Phillips later told club members that the huge shark made a grab at the boy as his flippers were breaking the water in a dive.

Mr. Phillips climbed on his surf ski and paddled over to the boy, whom he dragged from the blood-stained water. With the boy's body only half out of the water, he lashed it to the ski with a piece of plastic wire he was carrying, while at the same time beating off frenzied lunges by the shark. The battle lasted for ten minutes before Mr. Phillips could make for the shore with the shark still following and circling him.

In the meantime, Murray Bampton, a member of the Knights of Neptune Underwater Club, who had just brought a man with cramp to the shore, saw the struggle and went out on his surf ski to help. Mr. Bampton kept the shark away with his paddle, while Mr. Phillips continued in. When in a few feet of water, the two men carried the boy on Mr. Phillips' ski to the beach. Sister Heather Jones, who was on the beach, ran over to help.

Dr. R. J. de N. Souter of Yankalilla, who was summoned to the scene, pronounced the youth dead. It is understood that the boy's injuries were such that he would have died within thirty seconds of the attack. The boy had suffered shocking injuries to his right leg, extending from the calf muscles to half way up the thigh, and gashes to his left leg, all of which are believed to have been made in the shark's only bite.

Adelaide Advertiser, 10 December 1962

QUEENSLAND, AUSTRALIA, 1937

Norman Girvan, 18, of Coolangatta, was killed by a shark while surfing at the main beach at Coolangatta this afternoon.

Jack Brinkley, a youth, of Coolangatta, was badly mauled and later had his left arm amputated in hospital.

Joe Doniger showed great heroism in going to the help of Brinkley and bringing him ashore.

This is the first shark tragedy at Coolangatta.

Six members of the surf life-saving club, including Girvan, Brinkley, Joe Doniger and Gordon Doniger, went for their usual swim after work. The surf was choppy and storm clouds obscured the sun. After some time in the water, Joe Doniger and two others returned to the beach, leaving Girvan, Brinkley and Gordon Doniger about one hundred yards out in the surf. Shortly after they reached the beach—about 5:25 pm—the shark attacked Girvan, inflicting terrible wounds.

Gordon Doniger swam towards Girvan to help him, but Girvan was then so badly torn by the shark that he was beyond aid, and Gordon Doniger and Brinkley swam as fast as they could for the shore.

When Brinkley, who was leading, was about seventy-five yards from the beach, the shark attacked him, tearing his left shoulder and one leg. He screamed for help and Joe Doniger dashed into the surf and swam quickly to Brinkley's side. "For God's sake hurry up," cried Brinkley, and collapsed. The shark was still cruising near by, but Doniger seized Brinkley and brought him to the shore, where he and the others applied a tourniquet to the torn arm.

Alf Kilburn, one of the party, then went out a short distance on a surf ski to find Girvan's body. At the first line of breakers he saw the shark circling near a patch of blood-stained water and he returned to the beach. By this time the surf club's boat had been manned and several surfers went out in it. They searched for half an hour for Girvan's body without success. They saw no sign of the shark.

The shark was about ten feet long and either a tiger or grey nurse. Girvan was a member of the Kirra Surf Life-Saving Club for years and was one of its most popular members.

Sydney Morning Herald, 28 October 1937

3
Ships and Boats and Planes

NEW SOUTH WALES, AUSTRALIA, 1996

A group of Australian fishermen who underwent a nine-hour ordeal yesterday after a giant shark gnawed off the bow of their twenty-one-foot boat have vowed to stick to golf in future.

The three men and one woman were fishing off the coast of New South Wales and had fed one hundred litres of shark bait—mainly offal—into the sea when a fourteen-foot mako bit into the front of their fibreglass boat, the *Mini Haa Haar* [sic].

Tony Barnes, one of the fishermen, said: "We had just started fishing about eight miles off shore when the shark hit us. I saw his body pass the boat, and then suddenly he ploughed straight into the bow. In three minutes the boat went down."

With room on their tiny inflatable dinghy for only one, the others had to cling to the sides with their legs dangling in the sea. Tony Green, the skipper, said: "I could see the dorsal fin going round and round, circling us for about an hour and a half. Then, eventually, the shark lost interest. That was the last we saw of it, thank God."

After nine hours the group hailed a passing tanker, but could not attract anyone's attention. "There was nobody on watch on the ship and the crew appeared not to see us," said Barnes. They had to swim towards it towing Barnes's wife, Kylin, on the inflatable before they were finally picked up, shivering from cold and shock. They were then air-lifted to Wollongong hospital, near Sydney.

"We are doubly lucky to be alive," said Barnes, vowing to give up deep-sea fishing for golf. "I'm staying on land from now on and I'll buy my fish in a fish shop." The four were discharged from hospital after treatment for severe exposure and dehydration.

Sunday Times, London, 14 January 1996

CARIBBEAN SEA, GULF OF MEXICO, 1974

A mother whose life was devastated when sharks killed two of her children during a "perfect family holiday" in the Gulf of Mexico is still struggling twenty years later to come to terms with the tragedy.

She has not been able to stand on a beach since and her hatred of sharks has remained undiminished. Mrs. Horne, an American who says she relives the appalling experience every day of her life, is, with the help of wildlife experts from the American National Wildlife Foundation, trying to overcome her hatred of sharks.

On 2 July 1974, Diane and her husband Ed set off in a forty-three-foot motor boat for a 300-mile trip with their five children—Diana, 14, Gerald, 12, Billy, 10, Melissa, 4, and three-year-old Tex. The weather bureau had predicted a dry night with calm seas. Yet, within two hours of leaving Florida Harbour in Panama, a sudden storm smashed their boat to pieces and they were forced to leap into rough seas in pitch darkness. They managed to rope themselves together and floated about for several hours.

Diane recalled: "We felt very alone, just out there in the water and the night seemed to go on for ever."

The family, cold and exhausted, drifting in and out of sleep, were overjoyed in the early morning by the sound of a spotter plane. In their excitement they untied the rope to spread out in the water and began shouting. It was probably their biggest mistake, because the noise and disturbance alerted the sharks. "We saw a dorsal fin, but thought it was dolphin. All of a sudden we saw a rescue boat and were hit by the sharks at the same time," recalled Diane.

The family and screaming children thrashed the water with their legs and arms in a frantic attempt to keep the sharks at bay.

One by one the twelve-foot animals went on the attack. Their first target was Billy. Spiked teeth closed on him and the sea coloured with blood as part of his arm was torn off. Diane was pushed out of the water and the shark grazed her skin. The pilot in the aircraft reported seeing masses of sharks circling the family.

The arrival of a Coast Guard vessel saved the rest of the family from certain death. Her ten-year-old son Billy was badly savaged. Diane held him in her right arm, trying to staunch the gaping wound in his right arm, but he bled to death. Three-year-old Tex later died from exposure.

In a moving postscript Mrs. Horne said: "There is not a night that I have laid my head on the pillow that I haven't thought of this, but it wasn't until I got involved with the National Wildlife Foundation, which made me understand nature more, that I've been able to accept it. They weren't really out to kill someone. They were doing their thing and I was doing my thing, and the two worlds collided."

London Evening Standard, 6 September 1995

CALIFORNIA, USA, 1993

After being thrown from her kayak on to the body of a great white shark off the Sonoma coast last weekend, Rosemary Johnson has been taking life's little problems a bit less seriously. "I work in a restaurant where people get uptight if food is two minutes late," said Johnson, 34, who is a waitress in St. Helena. "Now, I tell them, 'Hey, it's only soup—it's not even a matter of survival.'"

Johnson said she experienced a spiritual renaissance after a giant shark exploded through the water of Bodega Bay, south of Goat Rock, gripping her narrow vessel and launching her ten feet in the air in front of four other panicked kayakers.

"I thought I had hit some kind of sandy rock," said Johnson, whose feet landed on the shark as it swam underneath her. "Then my friends started screaming and shouting. They were so frightened, and I didn't understand why."

Friends screamed to Johnson to get back into the kayak, which kept tipping over. When Johnson understood a shark was near by, she began to go into shock.

"At first I was too confused to be afraid, but when I kept falling into the water over and over, then I have to say I was scared."

In a rescue which seemed miraculous, friends helped Johnson get back into her kayak and to shore. The shark, which experts estimated from triangular teeth marks on the kayak to be fourteen to fifteen feet long and 1,000 to 1,500 lbs, never reappeared.

Johnson, who declined press interviews for several days after the attack, said she needed time to rethink her life. "I could have died. It changed my life. When I got back, I looked at my two kids and thought: wow, this is life, this is what's important—have fun, play."

Passing rangers from the Sonoma Coast State Beach checked Johnson for hypothermia, gave her a blanket and asked jokingly if she would like to buy them lottery tickets, she said.

A warning about the attack, the third along the Sonoma coast this year, has been posted for tomorrow along a ten-mile stretch of beach from the mouth of the Russian River to Bodega Head, said Brian Hickey, chief ranger for the Sonoma Coast State Beach.

Johnson said that she intends to continue kayaking and windsurfing in the ocean, but that she will never again separate from her group. "What is the chance of me getting attacked twice? That would be pretty amazing."

San Francisco Chronicle, 15 October 1993

CARIBBEAN SEA, GULF OF MEXICO, 1993

Two British brothers have arrived in Jamaica exhausted and starving after sharks attacked and damaged their canoe in the Caribbean, forcing them to abandon an attempt to become the first to paddle from Europe to mainland America.

Chris and Stuart Newman, from Middlesbrough, Cleveland, England, said yesterday that they clung to their capsized canoe for four hours in the middle of the night as sharks spun it round. By daylight the sharks had disappeared, but it was another five days before they came ashore on the sixty-eighth day of their attempt to cross from Portugal to Florida. The brothers are now recovering in hospital in Port Antonio, where they are being treated for malnutrition and salt-water boils.

Chris Newman, 32, said yesterday that the sharks were attracted by oil and blood seeping into the sea from a dolphin they caught south of the Dominican Republic on 4 January.

"We ran out of food on 23 December and the dolphin was to have been an excellent source of food. We butchered it and attached it to the canoe, but it attracted two white-tipped sharks," he said.

As one of the ten-foot sharks rubbed against the canoe, the brothers tried to scare it off by spearing it with a harpoon, but it dropped behind the canoe and was joined by another shark. They tore into the dolphin and damaged the canoe as they spun it round.

Stuart, 30, said: "We hung on for dear life. We could not right the canoe because that would have meant falling into the water again, so we waited for about four hours, for daylight, and by then the sharks were nowhere to be seen."

With no food and their navigation equipment destroyed, the brothers realised their record attempt was over. On Saturday they sighted Jamaica and early the next day they came ashore at Manchioneal, on the east of the island. But their ordeal did not end there. Chris said: "Starving and barely able to stand up, we found some coconuts to eat. When daylight came, a fisherman gave us some of his catch, but others tried to steal our equipment. But, since then, we have been well looked after in the hospital."

The brothers' canoe was so small, measuring 19 ft × 33 ins, that they could not take enough food for the crossing and had planned to rely on fish, but fishing was so bad that, after their food ran out on 23 December, they radioed a passing vessel for supplies.

The brothers, who are both former oil-riggers, will still go into the record books for travelling the furthest distance across the sea in the smallest boat. However, Chris said he was disappointed not to have made the crossing: "We will try again. We know we can cope physically in the ocean, but we need bigger sponsors."

Members of the brothers' family were less happy to hear they were contemplating another attempt after the failure of their third transatlantic crossing. Stuart's wife, Amanda, said, "I cannot order him to stop, but I will urge him to change tack. He has given me such a fright, but thank God he is alive." Their mother, Ada, added: "They have always been an adventurous pair and I just hope this will calm them down."

The Times, London, 13 January 1993

TUSCANY, ITALY, 1991

Shark fever has taken hold of the beaches of southern Liguria and northern Tuscany after a woman was attacked on Tuesday, while paddling her canoe off Portofino.

Ivana Iacaccia, aged forty, was left frightened, but unhurt, after managing to swim ashore while the shark savaged her canoe. Subsequent sightings of sharks by the Coast Guard and tourists in small boats have, however, kept shark fever high.

A shark hunt, led by Antonio Alati, a rear admiral in the Coast Guard service, is now under way. "We will try to kill the shark with the weapons that equip our control boats," he announced. While Coast Guard launches and light aircraft patrol the water south of Genoa, dozens of would-be shark hunters are taking to the sea, armed with everything from makeshift harpoons to sophisticated fishing tackle. Those intercepted by the Coast Guard or the police are being advised to keep out of the way. The sightings—three on Tuesday and one on Thursday—report a shark between twelve and sixteen feet long, large by Mediterranean standards. Most beaches have put up red flags to warn swimmers, mothers are keeping an eye on their children, and bathers, sailors and windsurfers are scarce.

The national press has given ample space to the attack and hunt. The serious *La Stampa* newspaper of Turin even carried the report on its front page. This may, of course, be a reflection on the lack of substance in the recent, supposedly important rumblings in Italian politics.

Shark attacks in the Mediterranean are relatively rare. About thirty have been recorded this century [up to 1974], of which thirteen were fatal. Seven of these took place off Italy, and the most recent was in 1989 in the Gulf of Baratti, when a scuba diver was attacked [see p. 39]. Marine biologists from Genoa University are examining the remains of Signora Iacaccia's canoe. Some believe the shark was a *smeriglio*, a native of the Mediterranean which rarely becomes aggressive.

The Times, London, 3 August 1991

HONG KONG, 1991

Closure of nearly half of Hong Kong's forty-one public beaches followed the recovery of a mainland Chinese fisherman's body, a government spokesman said on Saturday.

The body of the Chinese fisherman was found floating in the waters off Saikung, on the northeastern Kowloon peninsula on Friday with his right arm severed from what is believed to be a shark, police stated.

An elderly woman died from a shark attack in the vicinity on 8 June. In addition to those local beaches, eleven other public beaches on the southern coast of Hong Kong island have been closed for the weekend with warning signals being hoisted after several sharks were sighted there.

Agence France Presse, 29 June 1991

CALIFORNIA, USA, 1989

A woman apparently killed by a great white shark off the coast near Oxnard was identified on Monday as a UCLA student on a kayaking excursion with her boyfriend, who is still missing, authorities stated.

The two, both UCLA graduate students, had left Malibu on Thursday for a morning of kayaking, said Ventura County Sheriff Lt. Lary Reynolds. Both one-person kayaks were found on Friday five miles off the coast of Zuma Beach. One of the kayaks has three large holes that probably were punctures made by the teeth of a shark, said Reynolds.

Tamara McCallister, 24, of Mar Vista, was found on Saturday about six miles off Channel Island Harbor in Oxnard by the crew of a sailboat. Her companion, Roy Jeffrey Stoddard, 24, of Malibu, is a UCLA graduate student in epidemiology.

Randy Lee, who shared a Malibu beach house with Stoddard, said McCallister and Stoddard had dated for about a year. Both had evening classes at UCLA and frequently kayaked together in the morning. On the day they disappeared, Lee said, they took muffins and coffee out to the beach, had breakfast and then took off for a short trip. They planned to paddle to Paradise Cove—about one and a half miles away—and return.

"Roy knew there was a slow leak in his kayak, so there's no way he was planning on going any further than the cove," Lee said. "It was just a short trip and they did it all the time. Roy wasn't a reckless guy and he wouldn't do anything that would put himself in jeopardy. So I really think this shark business took place around here and the currents took them up the coast."

Stoddard "really knew the ocean," said Lee. He was an experienced scuba diver and surfer, and had been kayaking more than five years. After graduating from Pepperdine University in 1987 with honours, Stoddard, whose family lives in San Jose, entered graduate school at UCLA. He had recently applied to medical school, Lee added, and had just received his first acceptance letter.

McCallister moved to Los Angeles from Portland, Oregon, in September to study for a master's degree in public health at UCLA, according to her mother, Linda McCallister. She had spent time in Africa and had wanted to go back there "to help people." The mother, who said she last saw Tamara at Christmas, called her daughter "an outdoors type." She said Tamara and Stoddard "took a liking to each other" because of their mutual interest in the outdoors.

Laverne Dye, who had rented a room to McCallister in her Mar Vista home, said she was an experienced kayaker, was extremely fit, and swam or ran every day . . .

The search continued on Tuesday for the missing companion of Tamara McCallister, while news of her violent death stunned classmates and faculty members on the UCLA Westwood campus.

Members of Roy Stoddard's family were arriving at his Malibu home still hopeful that he would be found alive, even though it has been more than five days since he set out from Malibu on a short morning kayaking excursion. "My brother was an expert in the water and, if anybody can survive, he can," said Rod Stoddard, who said he planned to embark on his own boat to search for his older brother. "I'm going to find him."

Two Coast Guard boats and a helicopter are scouring the coastline between Ventura and Malibu for signs of Stoddard, whose kayak was found on Friday about five miles off Point Mugu. The kayaks had been lashed together, a common practice when kayakers stop to rest or swim. One of the kayaks had three large holes, probably put there by the impact of a great white shark, authorities said.

McCallister's body, found on Saturday about six miles off the Ventura County coast, was identified on Monday. Authorities speculate that her body drifted north with the current . . .

Rod Stoddard said that his brother Roy had

taught him to surf when he was a child, coaching him to stay calm when the waves grew frightening. "We both have tremendous respect for the ocean and the environment. You can never underestimate the powers of the ocean."

Tom Myers, a friend and neighbour of Stoddard, described him as a careful and skilful outdoorsman who was as fit as a professional lifeguard. The shark attack, Myers said, had to have happened "within sight of shore. They wouldn't have gone outside the kelp beds. They're too smart for that."

He and Stoddard had gone scuba diving together, but had never been concerned about shark attacks, Myers said. "The possibility was always very remote. It's like going snow skiing and worrying about the wolves."

Los Angeles Times, 31 January, 1 February 1989

DOMINICAN REPUBLIC, 1987

Rescue workers on Wednesday began recovering the corpses of dozens of refugees who were thrown from a capsized vessel and drowned or were torn apart by sharks, authorities said in Santo Domingo.

More than 100 of the estimated 160 Dominicans, possibly attempting illegal entry into the United States, aboard the forty-foot boat bound east toward Puerto Rico were missing and presumed dead after the Tuesday disaster, said Eugenio Cabral, Dominican civil defence director. The overcrowded vessel left Nagua, about sixty miles north of the capital on

the Atlantic coast, early on Tuesday. The boat
caught fire when its motor exploded and it capsized
in the tumult of attempts to douse the flames.

Five civil defence boats and several fishing boats
resumed a search for survivors at daybreak on
Wednesday. Three bodies were recovered, and Luis
Rolon, civil defence director for San Juan, said eighteen women and four men were in hospital suffering
from cuts, bruises, shock and burns. The remaining
thirty-five were rescued unharmed.

Rolon said a female survivor interviewed by a radio station said the vessel's captain was intoxicated
during the incident, and gas canisters aboard the
boat spilled at the time of the explosion, spreading
the flames.

Between forty and fifty sharks attacked the survivors as they clung to the wreckage or floated after
currents pulled them twenty miles off shore, said
Rolon, who accompanied Cabral on his flight. Rescuers in helicopters and fishermen in small boats
pulled some survivors from the water amid the
shark attack, Cabral said.

Ernesto Uribe, public affairs officer at the US Em-
bassy in Santo Domingo, said he saw pictures of the
accident scene taken from a civil defence aircraft
and that numerous sharks could be seen circling
bodies and survivors. "It was big herd of sharks. It
was an awful sight."

Many Dominicans attempt the ninety-mile
crossing of the treacherous Mona Passage to Puerto
Rico. One survivor told authorities that passengers
had paid the boat's operators from $200 to $600 to
make the trip . . .

Atlanta Journal & Constitution, 8 October 1987

FLORIDA, USA, 1984

Three men competing in a shark fishing tournament became bait themselves when a thunderstorm capsized their boat, tossing them into seas scattered with blood and fish to attract the undersea killers. The episode was "like a bad dream," William Anderson, 34, said on Monday. "It's hard to believe it happened."

Anderson, William McConnell, 30, and William E. Stevens, 34, survived on Sunday by pulling themselves into two five-foot-long coolers, where they bobbed in rough seas for five hours until being picked up by a passing boat whose captain heard their calls for help.

"The chests were bumped frequently by sharks just checking us out," said Anderson, owner of the eighteen-foot *Boatem*. "From the size of the dorsal fin we saw cutting through the water, the largest shark out there was well over ten feet long."

The three Orlando men were competing in the US Open Sharkfishing Tournament when the storm overturned their boat in the same waters where they had already tossed shark bait, a few miles off the north-east Florida coast.

"We didn't see many sharks, but we could see the swirls and movements in the water around us," Anderson said. "We were using bonita as bait and that is a very bloody fish. All our efforts at attracting them were definitely beginning to pay off. We definitely saw them at a distance of fifteen to twenty feet."

The adventure began when the men were forced out to sea, trying to outrun a thunderstorm which walloped north-east Florida. The storm "chased us off shore for fifteen miles as we were running from it, trying to find a way through all that electricity," he said. Finally they found a way through the storm and anchored, settling down for some serious shark fishing in quest of the $4,700 first prize. But strong waves suddenly grabbed the stern around 6 pm, capsizing the craft within two minutes.

"Then the hard part started," Anderson said. "We were caught by winds and current."

During the next half hour, the men struggled in three-foot waves, trying to climb into two large coolers which had held bait and sharks which had already been caught.

"I felt like something had rubbed up against my leg," McConnell said. "I've got very light scratches there, marks with equal distance between them. It appears to be from shark skin, either the tail or side of a shark."

The men were not in the coolers for long before more sharks drew closer, apparently following the scent of blood and fish oil.

New Orleans Times-Picayune, 3 July 1984

QUEENSLAND, AUSTRALIA, 1983

The skipper of a capsized shrimp boat said he watched helplessly as a shark dragged away his two crew members, one of them as he clutched her hand.

Ray Boundy, 28, skipper of the *New Venture*, told his tale a few hours after being rescued from Loaders Reef, forty-five miles north-east of Townsville. He had been in the sea off Australia's north-east coast for thirty-six hours.

Boundy said from his hospital bed that deckhand Dennis Patrick Murphy, 24, of Brisbane, and his cook Linda Anne Horton, 21, of Townsville, were attacked by a shark he estimated to be fifteen feet long as they clung to the capsized vessel. He said his boat capsized on Sunday night in heavy seas sixty miles out of Townsville.

"The deckie (Murphy) was on deck and jumped into the water, but Lindy and I were caught in the wheelhouse. We all ended up sitting on top of the upturned hull wondering what we were going to do," said Boundy. They clung to wreckage, which included a surfboard, a life ring and pieces of Styrofoam from shrimp boxes as the trawler sank.

Boundy said the shark approached on Monday night. "We weren't taking much notice of him, thinking that if we didn't antagonize him, he might leave us alone. He took a bite at my leg under the surfboard, so I kicked him with my other foot and he let go."

About ten minutes later the shark struck.

"He's got my leg, the bastard's got my leg," Boundy quoted Murphy as screaming.

"You're joking," I said. "But then I could see the blood coming to the surface through the water. I didn't know what to do. We'd been hanging together so well for so long . . . pushed ourselves so hard. I just didn't know how to deal with it because we had no dinghy. We had nothing to use as a tourniquet, even if we stopped the bleeding. The shark was still going to come back and I just didn't know what to do.

"The shark came back and I said to Smurf (Murphy), 'What do you want to do?' and he said, 'You bolt. Gather in all the stuff. Leave me,' and he swam off about four or five paces.

"Everything seemed to be going all right for a couple of hours. I got Lindy to get her spirits back up and we seemed to be travelling along all right, and I knew we'd get to the reef some time in the morning," said Boundy.

At about 4 am the shark struck again.

"Lindy was sitting in the sling of the lifebuoy when I saw him come along again. I was pretty sure he was the same shark this time. He came along as slow as you like beside me, then slewed around and grabbed Lindy around the arms and the chest.

"I was still holding her by the hand as he shook her about three or four times. She only let out one little squeal as soon as it hit and I knew almost instantly that she was dead."

New Orleans Times-Picayune, 27 September 1983

FLORIDA, USA, 1982

A ninety-foot government ocean-charting vessel was attacked by a sixteen-foot shark off the Florida coast last month and briefly disabled, the National Oceanic Survey said.

The *Heck*, headed for Key West with its sister ship *Rude* to search for and chart navigation hazards, sustained damaged oil seals and a burned out steering motor when the shark attacked the port propeller and rudder off Jacksonville, an agency spokesman said. The shark was killed instantly.

The ship's captain, Lt. Cmdr. Russell Arnold, reported that divers made temporary repairs and the vessel was able to make its way to Jacksonville, where a new steering motor was installed. "It's the first time to my knowledge that this has ever happened to one of the twenty-five charting vessels operated by the National Oceanic and Atmospheric Administration, a unit of the Commerce Department."

The ships, which docked on Thursday in Key West, search for navigation hazards by dragging a submerged wire between them. The findings are then noted on navigational charts issued by NOAA's ocean survey unit.

New Orleans Times-Picayune, 20 March 1982

ISLE OF WIGHT, UK, 1981

A 400-lb shark was killed yesterday as it leapt at a small fishing boat off the south coast. Two fishermen were injured and the boat was damaged when the shark landed across the deck.

The incident happened off the Isle of Wight. Mr. Ross Staplehurst, a local fisherman, had taken a party of anglers for a day's fishing in his twenty-three-foot boat, the *Albatross*. They were fishing for tope and skate when the thresher shark, thirteen feet long, was sighted about fifty yards away.

Mr. Staplehurst said: "It turned towards the boat and dived. Everything was quiet for a moment and we thought it had swum away. Then there was a great rushing noise and suddenly the shark came surging out of the water about five yards away.

"It landed across the boat, which is only nine feet wide, so its head and tail were sticking over each side. The impact nearly sank the boat and it killed the shark outright."

One of the fishermen was hit by the shark's tail and his nose was cut. Another had a bruised leg. The *Albatross* sailed back to Bembridge, Isle of Wight, where the shark is to be sold to fishmongers.

"I have fished these waters for ten years," said Mr. Staplehurst, "but have never seen a shark act like that. It just went berserk. I'm convinced it was attacking the boat."

The Times, London, 15 June 1981

BAHAMA ISLANDS, UK, 1980

Many of the bodies recovered from the Gulf Stream twenty miles from Freeport, Grand Bahama, where a DC-3 crashed killing all thirty-four aboard, were mutilated in shark-infested waters, authorities said. The Coast Guard found sixteen bodies on Friday and Saturday, and suspended the search for more victims on Sunday. A Coast Guard spokesman

Great white shark approaching shark cage, Australia
(Chuck Davis)

View from front: sand tiger shark with jaws open *(Jeff Rotman)*

hortfin mako shark eating tuna bait, South Pacific
Darryl Torckler)

Close-up of sand tiger shark's mouth *(Jeff Rotman)*

Great white shark, Australia *(Stuart Westmorland)*

Great white shark with divers in protective cage, South Australia *(Jeff Rotman)*

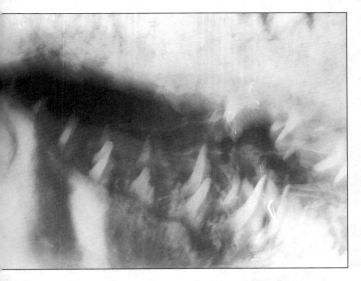

Shark, close-up of jaws covered in blood *(Nicholas DeVore)*

White-tip reef shark swimming over coral, Hawaii
(Mike Severns)

said there was no chance any of the other eighteen people aboard survived.

Autopsies by assistant Broward County Medical Examiner Sashi Gore showed some of the victims had been mangled by sharks. Many apparently drowned and others died of multiple injuries. The plane was equipped with life preservers, but none of the passengers were wearing them.

A fisherman who reportedly witnessed the crash at 9 pm on Friday, told Federal Aviation Administration officials the plane was on fire and "flaming like a meteorite" when it crashed into fifty feet of water.

Two Coast Guard cutters and two helicopters conducted a ten-hour search in the Bahamian seas. The captain of the cutter *Current*, Lt. Susan Moritz, 26, said the seas were four to six feet high and the wind was blowing out of the south-east at sixteen miles per hour.

The Florida Commuter Airlines plane crashed while making its final approach to Freeport in a violent thunderstorm. It was carrying passengers to Freeport casinos for a gambling excursion . . .

New Orleans Times-Picayune, 15 September 1980

INDIAN OCEAN, 1975

Mr. Valery Kosyak, a mechanic in the Soviet Union's Black Sea merchant fleet, has survived a four-hour ordeal among sharks. Mr. Kosyak, who is twenty-five and married with two children, was swept overboard from a cargo ship during a storm in the Indian Ocean 600 miles south of Sri Lanka, and found himself surrounded by a shoal of man-eaters.

"At first, when I felt something brushing at my legs, I thought it was driftwood," he said. "But then I was hit hard and turned over in the water. When I opened my eyes, I saw this pig-like snout sticking out of the sea in front of me. Then it dipped and disappeared."

The sharks, which surrounded him, were between nine and fifteen feet long. "They were diving in and out of the waves, and I tried to float flat on the water so they wouldn't go for my feet," Mr. Kosyak said. "They kept circling about fifteen feet away from me. When I realised they weren't going to attack immediately, I began to think a bit more clearly.

"They moved with me. I didn't hurry because it was obvious I could never shake them off. I knew I just had to keep up my strength until the ship came back, as I knew it would."

As he swam, he found himself talking to the sharks. "I was swearing and then cooing at them. I was steering myself by the sun, although it was pretty difficult to keep on course because I was swimming into the waves. Still, it helped me forget the sharks."

Two hours went by before his shipmates noticed that he was missing. The ship immediately turned back and found him after another two hours.

When M. Jacques-Yves Cousteau, the French underwater explorer, was asked to comment on Mr. Kosyak's ordeal, he said: "I have heard of people surviving an hour or two among sharks, but four hours—never."

The Times, London, 26 July 1975

WESTERN PACIFIC, 1970

Fourteen passengers were devoured by sharks when a motor launch capsized 200 miles south-east of Manila in the Philippines, police reported. Only a honeymoon couple survived out of the twenty-two on board. Six were drowned.

The Times, London, 24 September 1970

GIBRALTAR, 1967

It is the lonely distinction of Mr. Bernard Venables, a sixty-year-old fisherman and writer, to have had a tooth knocked out by a shark.

Off Gibraltar with two friends last month, he had a bite from a 143-lb shark and they managed, while he still held the rod, to get it into the boat. "It is very unwise," Mr. Venables recalled ruefully, "to bring a shark of that size into a small boat—ours was only a twenty-four-footer." But they got it in.

"And then it suddenly became very active. The back end hit one of my friends on the leg, so that he had to go straight to hospital. The front end gave me

117

a wallop on the head and knocked my pipe out of my mouth.

"At the time I was chiefly concerned that I was going to lose the pipe." (He recovered it.) "It was only when I got back and looked in the mirror that I realized I'd lost a tooth. Right in the middle, I'm afraid."

One of Mr. Venables's many books is *The Gentle Art of Angling*.

The Times, London, 15 May 1967

INDIAN OCEAN, 1959

A three-year-old child died and a woman was injured by sharks which attacked seventeen Maldivians who spent thirty-one days adrift in an open boat off the coast of Ceylon [Sri Lanka]. The islanders were rescued by the 20,500-ton Japanese tanker *Obminesan Maru*, which has reached Colombo.

The boat and its passengers were swept off course while crossing from one atoll to another in the Maldivian archipelago.

The Times, London, 14 December 1959

GULF OF MEXICO, 1959

The oil slick was four miles wide. Bodies and a life raft bobbed in it. Somewhere under it was the tomb of an undetermined number of persons on the National Air Line missing DC-7B. The big four-engine plane must have hit with a terrific impact. All of the clothing was torn from the bodies and the debris was in tiny pieces.

This reporter hitched a ride on a Coast Guard helicopter and arrived over the scene about 100 miles south-east of New Orleans at 11:30 am yesterday. There were no large pieces of the plane and, even though the sea was very clear, we could not see it in the water. The first thing I spotted was a partially inflated, yellow life raft belonging to the missing plane. It bobbed in the oil slick, which was ever widening. Further on there was a smoke signal floating as well as several yellow die markers, all dropped by other planes.

The first body I saw was an elderly, grey-haired man of heavy build with bruises on his back. His clothing was sort of purple and just hanging on him. Later we spotted another man. He was younger with blond hair and a good build, like an athlete. He was nude, but his body did not appear to be damaged externally. The next was a woman. Her blouse was up around her neck and that was all the clothing left on her. Before we left, the Coast Guard had recovered eight bodies and there appeared to be three more in sight.

Just as we turned to leave, we spotted the body of another woman. Beneath it was something big and grey. At first I thought it was another body. But, no, it was a ten-foot shark.

I shouted to the crewman of the helicopter, and he confirmed it, to my horror. It was worrying the body, which appeared to be torn up. I saw one gaping hole in the back.

I have never seen anything like that. I was ready to head for home.

Searchers held slim hope late yesterday that any passengers would be found alive from the giant airliner which crashed into the Gulf of Mexico. Forty-two persons were aboard. Nine bodies in tattered remains of clothing and small pieces of plane debris were picked up by the searchers . . .

Searchers combed the oil-slicked Gulf throughout the day. A grey dense coat of fog hung over the current, pushed by a steady wind. The Coast Guard halted the search at nightfall, but left two vessels in the area. The crash site, the Coast Guard said, probably would be marked off to aid salvage operations, but it would be difficult because of the water's depth.

One searching ship came across mail and clothing. The wind spread the debris—pieces of foam rubber and other interior plane parts—over a three- or four-mile area. The Coast Guard estimated the plane was in fifty fathoms of water.

A ten-foot shark was the only sign of life spotted in the wreckage area.

New Orleans Times-Picayune, 17 November 1959

MADEIRA, PORTUGAL, 1956

A shark attacked and sank a fishing boat, drowning a twenty-three-year-old fisherman, Manuel Pereira, off Funchal, Madeira.

The Times, London, 27 June 1956

ISLE OF MAN, UK, 1954

The threshing tail of a twenty-foot shark, which was brought on board in the nets of a Fleetwood trawler off the Isle of Man, struck a deckhand and broke his arm.

The Times, London, 7 October 1954

HONG KONG, 1954

Able Seaman James Cook of HMS *Comus*, who lived in Highbury, London, has died from an attack by a shark in Junk Bay, Hong Kong. An unusual number of sharks and giant rays are reported in the colony waters this summer.

The Times, London, 17 September 1954

SINGAPORE, 1954

A British sailor who was diving into the harbour at Singapore yesterday, helping the police to recover jettisoned packets of opium, was seized by a shark and has since died of his injuries.

The Times, London, 29 July 1954

PACIFIC OCEAN, 1945

On Monday, 30 July 1945, at five minutes past mid-night, four days after the USS *Indianapolis*, flagship of the massive Pacific Fifth Fleet, delivered the com-ponents of the Hiroshima bomb to Tinian, and just a few weeks before VJ Day, she was torpedoed by a Japanese submarine and sank within fifteen minutes. Of the 1,196 men on board, approximately 400 went down with the ship and 800 safely aban-doned her. Of these 800 men in the water, only 316 survived. This was America's greatest wartime sea disaster; partly due to the secrecy surrounding her course, the US Navy left her crew drifting in shark-infested waters for four days. The following account is taken from *All The Drowned Sailors* by Raymond B. Lech, largely based on the first-hand accounts of survivors:

[Monday, 30 July]
During this first day, a monstrous shark decided to investigate Captain McVay's raft and its edible cargo. The shark kept swimming under the raft. The dorsal fin was "almost white as a sheet of paper," while the body was a darker colour. The shark could therefore always be spotted because of the visibility of its white fin in the water. The frightened men attempted to catch some pilot fish by knocking them off with canoe paddles, but this was an exercise in

futility. They also tried hitting the shark with paddles, but, when they occasionally did manage to do so, he swam away and returned a few minutes later. In the days to follow, this unwanted nuisance was to become a real menace.

During the entire time in the water, Captain McVay's wrist-watch kept excellent time. At 1 pm a high-flying twin-engine bomber flew overhead in the direction of Leyte; at 3 pm either a B-24 or B-29 passed to the south of them, also heading for the Philippines . . . After spotting two distant rafts, McVay and the others in his group assumed that they were the sole survivors of the ship and, all in all, figured no more than twenty-five or thirty men, including themselves, had made it off the ship. What they did not know at the time was that they had drifted seven to ten miles north of the main groups.

Stranded in the middle of the deep and seemingly neverending Philippine Sea, the Captain understandably became very depressed. He daydreamed about taking a bath, drinking a cocktail and relaxing in comfort, and in the midst of such thoughts he wished to live, but soon reality broke in upon his fantasies . . .

Two hours prior to the close of their first day a plane flew overhead, its red-and-green running lights clearly visible. McVay fired one of the star shells skyward, but it went unnoticed . . .

Most of the men [in a group out of sight of McVay] were unrecognisable since they were black from the heavy fuel oil blanketing the water. It burned their eyes, clogged their nostrils and choked their throats. Lieutenant McKissick was part of this group . . .

Soon after the ship went down, there was an underwater explosion which was heard and felt by everyone. McKissick ordered the men around him to lie prone in order to raise their bodies as far out of the water as possible and lessen the concussion if there were any further blasts.

At approximately 1:30 am [just over an hour after the ship sank] Quartermaster 1st Class Robert Gause spotted a fin. By estimating the distance between the dorsal and tail, he guessed the shark to be about twelve feet long.

Quite a few sailors in his group were critically wounded. There were a large number of severe flash burns of the face, arms and body, and some men had compound fractures of one sort or another. There were no medical supplies of any kind for the frustrated Dr. Haynes, and many of the men with fractures and burns died from shock during the first few hours. After removing their life jackets, the dead were allowed to slip away. Before the boiling sun rose over the distant horizon that Monday morning about fifty of the original 400 were dead . . .

By daybreak this mass of floating humanity had split into three subgroups. The largest group contained about 200 men, the second 100 and the smallest about 50. These subgroups were separated from each other by a distance of only several hundred yards at most. Leader of the group of 200 men was Captain Edward Parke, Commanding Officer of the Marine Detachment and holder of the Bronze Star for bravery on Guadalcanal . . .

The main objective was for everyone to stay together. Captain Parke found a cork life ring with about 100 feet of attached line. To prevent drifting, he strung the line out and each man grabbed a piece of it and took up the slack. In this way they formed a long line which began to curl on itself, as a waggon train would circle against attack. The wounded were brought into the middle and tied to the life ring itself by the strings on their life jackets. There was no confusion and the men stayed well grouped together. If someone did drift off the line, Parke swam over to the man and herded him back in. On several occasions he gave his life jacket to a man without one and swam unsupported until he could find another . . .

[During] the first day there was constant change among the three subgroups. They would merge for a short time, then break apart again. The wounded stayed in fairly good shape and only a few men died. In order to determine death, Dr. Haynes would place his finger on the pupil of an eye and, if there was no reflex, it was assumed the man was dead. The jacket would be removed and the body allowed to drift away. In the background some of the men would recite the Lord's Prayer.

By noontime the sea became choppy again with large swells . . . The survivors were beginning to see sharks in the area, but, so far, there were no major attacks. Giles McCoy of the Marine detachment saw a shark attack a dead man. He believed that, because of the dead men in the water, so much food was available that the sharks were not inclined to bother with those still alive at this stage.

That, however, had been in the morning and afternoon. By the time that the merciless sun began to set, large numbers of sharks had arrived on the scene, and the men were scared. Cuts were bleeding. When a shark approached a group, everyone would kick, punch and create a general racket. This often worked and the predator would leave. At other times, however, the shark "would have singled out his victim and no amount of shouts or pounding of the water would turn him away. There would be a piercing scream and the water would be churned red and the shark cut his victim to ribbons . . ."

At dawn on the second day the isolated Redmayne group had about sixty men on rafts and another sixty to eighty in the water. Meanwhile, during the dark morning hours, some of the more seriously injured men had died.

The water breakers turned out to be a disappointment. Some of the casks were empty, while the others contained either salt or cruddy black water . . . First-aid equipment was generally useless, since the containers were not watertight. Anything in tubes remained sealed, but there were not enough remedies to go around for burns and eye troubles caused by salt water and fuel oil. The food stayed in good condition, but, here again, there was a problem since the primary staple was Spam. Not only did this increase thirst because it was salty but also Spam draws sharks. The men discovered this when they opened a can of Spam and sharks gathered all around them.

The policy of the group was to put all men on rafts

who were sick, injured or did not have life jackets or belts. The problem with this, however, was that men with belts or jackets began taking them off and allowing them to drift away in order to qualify for the relative safety of a raft. This necessitated keeping a close watch on the men . . .

As far as can be ascertained, there were no deaths in this group during the second day, and everyone appeared to be in fairly good shape . . . The next day would be a different story . . .

Even though total blackness surrounded them [during the night of Monday–Tuesday], because of the choppy sea the men [in Haynes's group] were having a very difficult time sleeping. In this inky isolation some of the weaker members of the crew, who could not face what they thought must be ahead of them, gave up all hope: they silently slipped out of their life jackets and committed suicide by drowning. Numerous deadly fights broke out over life jackets and about twenty-five men were killed by their shipmates. At dawn Dr. Haynes saw that the general condition of the men was not good, and the group appeared to be smaller . . .

During the latter part of [Tuesday] the sea grew calmer. The men's thirst, however, had become overpowering as the placid water became very clear. As the day wore on the men became more and more exhausted and complained of thirst. Dr. Haynes noticed that the younger men, largely those without families, started to drink salt water first. As the hot sun continued to beat down on them, an increasing number of survivors were becoming delirious, talking incoherently and drinking tremendous amounts of salt water. They started becoming maniacal, thrashing around in the water and exhibiting considerable strength and energy compared to those who were exhausted but still sane . . .

Haynes kept swimming from one huge huddle of sailors to another, desperately trying to help. All during this time people were getting discouraged and calling out for help, and he would be there to reassure and calm them down.

There were sharks in the area again. The clear water allowed the men to look down and see them. It seems that during this second day, however, the sharks were going after dead men, especially the bodies that were sinking down into the deeper ocean. They did not seem to bother the men on the surface.

Things became progressively worse from sundown on the second day. The men's stories become mixed up, and some accounts are totally incoherent, making it difficult to piece together what actually happened. Haynes remembered that shortly after sundown they all experienced severe chills, which lasted for at least an hour. These were followed by high fever, as most of the group became delirious and got out of control. The men fought with one another, thinking there were Japanese in the group, and disorganization and disintegration occurred rapidly . . .

The Captain and the men with him were continuing to fare relatively well [by Wednesday 1 August]. McVay still believed that his ship went down with all hands and that, at most, there would only be thirty survivors.

From the opening of this [the third] day the central thought on the minds of the men was to kill the shark; it was big, it kept circling closer and closer, and they were frightened. This monster could easily rip the raft apart with one swift motion of his enormous jaws. But the only weapon they had was a knife from the fishing kit with a one-inch blade, and there was no way they could tackle this massive creature with a blade that small. So the day passed with the men sitting and staring at the shark, annoyed that a larger weapon was not in the kit and further chafed that not one man had a sheath knife, an implement customarily carried by many of the sailors aboard ship.

Just before first light a plane flew over and two star shells were fired. Again at 1 pm a bomber, heading towards Leyte, passed above. They tried to attract this second plane with mirrors, yellow signal flags and splashing, but to no avail. They were becoming more and more depressed since it did not seem possible to them that somebody they could see so plainly could fail to see them . . . Many aircraft flew close to the area where the ship sank. Each day planes were seen, but they all failed to spot the survivors. The glassy sea made it almost impossible to spot something as small as a man's head, and the chance of life rafts being picked up on radar was negligible unless the rafts were equipped with metal corner reflectors, which the rafts on the *Indianapolis* were not . . .

Although the order had been given the day before to bring all food to the command raft, there was still a certain amount of hoarding going on. This morning, however, several more rafts handed their cached rations over to Redmayne. During the day one cracker, a malted milk tablet and a few drips of precious water were allocated to each man. Some survivors tried their luck at fishing, but, as with the McVay group, the numerous sharks in the area kept stealing the bait.

Not everyone realized there was safety in numbers. Some men swam away. Attempts to stop them failed and soon after leaving the security of the group these sailors were usually dragged beneath the surface by the sharks . . .

Toward late afternoon some of the sailors started becoming delirious again. More and more men were drinking salt water. Chief Benton, Redmayne's assistant, attempted to talk to these half-crazed men in a calm, reassuring voice, but it was not much use. Fights broke out, men started swimming away and people committed suicide by drowning themselves . . .

Dr. Haynes's group disbanded again. Small groups were continually forming and breaking up. The night had been particularly difficult, and most of the men suffered from chills, fever and were delirious. These lonely people were now dying in droves and the helpless physician could only float and watch. By Thursday morning, 2 August, the condition of most of the men was critical. Many were in coma and could be aroused only with exceptional effort. The group no longer existed, with the men drifting off and dying one by one . . .

At dawn, a sailor in a life jacket was seen bent over with his face in the water. Thinking him asleep, a shipmate swam over to waken the man. On attempting to rouse him, the body flipped over and from the waist down there was nothing. He had been sawed clean in half by a shark.

At 9 am, on Thursday 2 August, securely strapped in the pilot's seat, Lieutenant Wilbur C. Gwinn pushed the throttles forward, brought the motors of his twin-engine Ventura bomber to an ear-splitting roar and raced down the Peleliu runway. His mission was a regular day reconnaissance patrol of sector 19V258. The route for the outward leg of his journey just happened to have him flying directly over the heads of the dying men of the *Indianapolis* . . .

At 11 am, about an hour and forty-five minutes out of Peleliu, Gwinn happened to look down from his 3,000-foot perch into the Philippine Sea. At that precise moment, he saw it. The thin line of oil could only have come from a leaking submarine, and the startled pilot rushed back to his left-hand seat and began flying the airplane.

At 11:18 am he changed his course so as to follow the snakelike slick. Not being able to see very well, he brought the bomber down to 900 feet. Five miles later he [saw wreckage and survivors] . . .

Looking down at the bobbing mass of humanity, he knew they were in horrible shape, but also just as important—and maybe even more so—he saw the sharks. Therefore, at "about 16:30 I decided a landing would be necessary to gather in the single

ones. This decision was based partly on the number
of single survivors and the fact that they were bothered by sharks. We did observe bodies being eaten
by sharks." Marks told [the control at his base] that
the Dumbo was landing and that he himself needed
relief . . .

Before night fell Marks had picked up thirty people and crammed them into the body of his leaking
seaplane. All were in bad shape, and they were immediately given water and first aid. Naturally, as
soon as the first man was plucked from the sea,
Lieutenant Marks learned that the *Indianapolis*
had gone down. There was no way, however, that he
was going to transmit this word in the clear, and "I
was too busy to code a message of this nature." So
it would not be until Friday 3 August that the US
Navy finally learned that one of their heavy cruisers
had been sunk just after midnight on 30 July . . .

For miles around the sea carried corpses. The many
destroyers on the scene served as funeral directors.
Because the sharks had been at work, identification
was next to impossible.

The search lasted six days, covering hundreds of
square miles of ocean. The result was always the
same—bodies, bodies and more bodies.

In his action report Commander A. F. Hollings-
worth, Captain of the USS *Helm*, brought into stark
reality how hideous the discovering of bodies really
was:

"All bodies were in extremely bad condition and
had been dead for an estimated four or five days.
Some had life jackets and life belts, most had nothing. Most of the bodies were completely naked, and

the others had just drawers or dungaree trousers on—only three of the twenty-eight bodies recovered had shirts on. Bodies were horribly bloated and decomposed—recognition of faces would have been impossible. About half of the bodies were shark-bitten, some to such a degree that they more nearly resembled skeletons. From one to four sharks were in the immediate area of the ship at all times. At one time two sharks were attacking a body not more than fifty yards from the ship and continued to do so until driven off by rifle fire. For the most part it was impossible to get fingerprints from the bodies as the skin had come off the hands or the hands had been lacerated by sharks . . . There were still more bodies in the area when darkness brought a close to the gruesome operations for the day."

All the other ships of the scouting flotilla were performing the same revolting task as *Helm* . . .

The sharks had been having a feast. When a boat reached a body, it was common to see a hand missing or foot gone, a part of the head ripped off, or a chunk of meat torn from the torso. It was also usual to find nothing but bones.

In two days the USS *French* examined twenty-nine bodies, but could not identify eighteen (sixty-two per cent) of them. The *French*'s report monotonously repeated over and over again: "Impossible to take fingerprints," "Body badly decomposed," "Very badly mutilated by sharks."

As the evening sun dropped over the western horizon on Wednesday 8 August 1945 the ships sailed for home, leaving in their wake the graveyard of the USS *Indianapolis* and the final burial ground of seventy-three per cent of her young crew.

HONG KONG, 1938

W. M. Baker, a sailor on HMS *Folkestone*, has died
on board the warship *Tsingtao* after his leg had been
bitten off by a shark while he was swimming near
the vessel in the outer harbour.

The Times, London, 30 August 1938

SCOTLAND, 1937

A large shark leapt out of the water in Carradale
Bay, Kintyre, last night and holed a fishing boat,
drowning three of the five occupants.

The victims were: Captain Angus Brown; his
brother, Robert, a fisherman of Carradale; and his
son Neil, aged ten. Captain Brown's twelve-year-old
daughter and a local youth, Donald McDonald, were
found clinging to the side of the sinking boat, the
girl holding with one hand the body of her father.

Holidaymakers on the shore saw the shark leap
high out of the water and the fishing boat disappear.
The body of the boy, Neil, was found some distance
from the boat, where it had been thrown by the
charge of the shark. The bodies of Captain Brown
and his son were taken to the pier. Meanwhile boats
searched the bay for the body of Robert Brown,

which had not been recovered at a late hour last night.

Large shoals of basking sharks, which measure up to thirty feet and weigh over six tons, have been in the Firth of Clyde for some days past and have been causing havoc among fishermen's nets. These sharks are generally considered harmless in that they do not normally attack human beings, but their weight and power when they leap out of the water make them a menace to fishing boats and other small craft.

The Times, London, 2 September 1937

SCOTLAND, 1937

A second attack by a basking shark on a fishing boat in the Firth of Clyde occurred early on Saturday when the *Lady Charlotte* of Campbeltown (twenty tons) was damaged off the Fallen Rocks, Arran.

The *Lady Charlotte*, which is owned by Messrs. Neil McKenzie & Co., Campbeltown, had secured a catch of herrings off the Arran coast and was on her way to Ayr to market the fish when a member of the crew, who was near the stern, saw a huge shark charge at the boat. The shark struck the propeller a glancing blow. The stern of the boat was lifted three feet out of the water by the impact and came down again with a crash, fortunately on an even keel. The crew saw the shark pass underneath their keel at an angle and, as it disappeared, they were able by

the gleam of the mast lights to follow its trail for
some time.

Mr. Colin McSporran, the skipper of the *Lady
Charlotte*, said that if the shark had caught the boat
a straight blow amidships, instead of merely a
glancing blow on the propeller, the boat would have
been sunk. The propeller shaft was smashed by the
shark's charge and the engines thrown out of gear.
It was with great difficulty that the vessel, after her
catch had been dumped, was able to limp into Campbeltown harbour.

The previous attack by a basking shark was on
the fishing boat *Eagle*, in Carradale Bay, Kintyre,
last Wednesday, when three men were drowned.

The Times, London, 6 September 1937

SCOTLAND, 1937

Another incident indicating the manner in which
navigation of the estuary of the Clyde by small vessels is being menaced by the presence of large numbers of basking sharks occurred last night. The
pleasure steamer *Glen Sannox* was crossing from
Ardrossan to Arran with many weekend holidaymakers when a shark struck the vessel. Two windows of the cabin were smashed. Some of the
passengers were rather scared when they heard the
crash, but beyond the damage to the windows no
harm was done.

Fishermen in the Firth assert that the attacks on
small vessels are being made by the blue predatory

shark, which has not been seen in these waters for at least forty years, and not by basking sharks, which are harmless and are frequently seen in the Clyde.

The Times, London, 13 September 1937

NOUMEA, NEW CALEDONIA, 1936

At the Marine Board offices in Cardiff last week the Lord Mayor of Cardiff, Alderman G. F. Evans, presented the Bronze Medal and Certificate of the Royal Humane Society to G. J. Butterworth, an apprentice of the steamer *Great City*, owned by Messrs. Sir W. R. Smith & Sons, Cardiff, for diving into a shark-infested sea at Noumea and swimming round the ship in order to rescue a seaman who had fallen overboard. The owners also presented a cheque for £50 and a gold watch.

The captain of the steamer, in a letter to the owners, stated that seven sharks were seen near the ship at the time and they were kept at bay by coal flung at them from the ship in order to disturb the water. Otherwise the seaman and Butterworth would probably have been attacked.

The Times, London, 9 July 1936

PANAMA, CENTRAL AMERICA, 1925

In April of last year the New Zealand Shipping Company's steamer *Dorset* picked up a seaman who had fallen overboard from the American tank steamer *Fred W. Weller* twenty-two hours previously. Under the command of Captain C. R. Kettlewell, the *Dorset* was leaving the Panama Canal bound for Auckland, New Zealand, and at 2:30 am, when eighteen miles from land, a cry for help was heard from the water.

The captain turned the ship in a circle in the hope of locating the man, although the night was intensely dark. A lifebuoy was dropped with a flare attached, and the man was seen and rescued.

He turned out to be Cleomont L. Staden of Brooklyn and stated that he had been twenty-two hours in the water, supported by a lifebuoy which was thrown when he fell overboard during the night. He said that he was frequently attacked by sharks and that water snakes had repeatedly crawled over him. He had kept the sharks at bay by beating the water with a piece of driftwood, which he still held when rescued. Although much exhausted, he soon recovered . . .

The Times, London, 13 October 1925

WEYMOUTH, UK, 1924

A man-eating shark twelve feet long was caught by Weymouth fishermen who were netting mackerel on Sunday. The shark broke two men's arms with its tail before it was hauled into the boat.

The Times, London, 15 July 1924

WESTERN AUSTRALIA, AUSTRALIA, 1910

An account reached Plymouth, UK, yesterday of a ship's crew having been devoured by sharks. Theodore Anderson was engaged in a pearling schooner on the Australian coast, when, during a storm, the vessel drove ashore between Broome and Fremantle. All the men with the exception of Anderson and the captain put off in the ship's boats, which capsized one by one, the men being eaten by sharks. The captain tried to reach the shore, but was seized before the eyes of Anderson, who eventually swam ashore.

The Times, London, 24 December 1910

4
Swimming out of one's Depth

It seemed a perfect start to the day as Jean Hotchkiss padded across a deserted shore and waded into
the clear water. Dawn was breaking over the Australian resort of Heron Island as the British holidaymaker lazily swam in the sea surrounding the
Great Barrier Reef.

Then terror struck in the shape of a shark "with
a mouth as wide as a chair." Before she could react,
it opened its jaws and tore into her arm and leg.
With blood pouring from her wounds, forty-seven-
year-old Miss Hotchkiss frantically swam back to
shore with her good arm, screaming for help and
praying the shark would not attack again.

Yesterday, after four hours of surgery in a Brisbane hospital, the landowner from Warwickshire,
England, told of her ordeal.

"I had been on the island a week and I was just

enjoying my usual early morning swim, doing a gentle breast stroke, not splashing around, when I looked down to my right. A chill went through me when I saw this huge shark next to me. The only thing I could see was this big, grey head. I was horrified, but before I could do anything, I felt its teeth ripping into my arm. I thought, my God, I've been bitten, and I started shouting: 'Help, help, somebody help me.' As I did that, the shark let me go.

"I was so shocked I just started swimming away as fast as I could. My biggest fear was that it would come back and take me out to sea. I looked at my arm and it was in shreds."

Despite almost fainting with fear, Miss Hotchkiss staggered 200 yards back to her hotel, banging on doors, shouting for help. She lost nearly three pints of blood.

"I managed to get to the reception and they got the nurse," she said. "Luckily there was an American doctor on holiday there and he organised a tourniquet. I was cold and shocked."

Shivering in her wet bikini and wrapped in blankets, Miss Hotchkiss was flown by helicopter to a local hospital at Rockhampton. There she was patched up and transferred to Brisbane by the Royal Flying Doctor Service. There, twelve hours after the attack, doctors repaired severed tendons and carried out skin grafts. They are confident she will regain full use of her arm.

Miss Hotchkiss, a fan of the *Jaws* movies, had swum with harmless reef sharks in Heron harbour days earlier. Experts believe her attacker was a tiger shark. She said: "I think my experience should be a warning to other people not to swim at dawn or dusk when sharks are feeding. I'm lucky to be alive."

Miss Hotchkiss, who lives off rent from the family estate near Stratford-upon-Avon, has a boyfriend, but spends a lot of time travelling alone. Her next adventure will be a cruise on the *Canberra* to Venice in August. "I'll need a holiday after all this," she laughed. "The streets of Venice may be under water, but at least there are no sharks."

Daily Mail, London, 9 March 1996

Editor's Note: Unfortunately Miss Hotchkiss is mistaken. Despite the perhaps inevitable secrecy surrounding shark attacks in the Mediterranean (particularly when they involve tourists in well-known resorts), and the extreme reluctance of research institutes and local authorities to supply information on recent attacks in the region, such attacks are becoming increasingly common. Two reports of attacks in Italian waters are given in previous chapters (pp. 39 and 102). As long ago as 1974, H. David Baldridge in his book *Shark Attack* gave the following figures for *reported* attacks: African coast 1, Egypt 4, Greece 4, Italy 7, Israel 1, Malta 1, and what was formerly Yugoslavia 12. And see below . . .

MEDITERRANEAN, 1967

Dr. P. H. Greenwood of the Natural History Museum, London, with whom this paper spoke yesterday about the report of sharks in the Bay of Naples, tells us that there are some 200 sorts of shark and that many of them live and breed in the Mediterranean. It is the comparatively cool temperature of the water which makes them mostly harmless. But attacks have been recorded at Valletta [see below], Fiume [see below], the Piraeus, Corfu and Genoa.

Little is known, as he says, about what makes a shark attack a man. It will single out a particular swimmer among a crowd and pursue him. Statistics show that sharks do not discriminate between sex or colour. It was thought at one time that sharks preferred Englishmen to Frenchmen because of some attractive odour emitted by the beefeating race which became apparent in the water, but modern records no longer support this theory!

The Times, London, 15 June 1967

VALLETTA, MALTA, 1956

Mr. Jack Smedley, a technical instructor at the British dockyard technical school, was killed by a shark today while he was swimming with a Maltese friend.

The Times, London, 21 July 1956

ITALY/CROATIA (YUGOSLAVIA), 1954

A large shark was seen in the sea close to Duino Castle, the residence at Trieste of General Winterton, the [post-war] zone commander, yesterday. Police launches patrolled the area and bathers were warned to keep near the shore. A few days ago a Hungarian refugee who swam to zone A from zone B reported that another refugee who had been swimming with him had been eaten by a shark.

The Times, London, 16 July 1954

YUGOSLAVIA, 1935

At Susak, near Fiume [now known as Rijeka, Istria] on Monday a girl bather was killed by a shark.

The Times, London, 3 July 1935

HONG KONG, 1995

A second man has died in a suspected shark attack in Hong Kong, sparking fears that a killer shark was stalking the annual Dragon Boat Festival which drew huge crowds to the colony's beaches on Friday.

A police spokeswoman said that the latest victim, identified as Herman Lo Cheuk-Yuet, was swimming with friends off Sheung Sze Wan beach in the New Territories when he was dragged under and mauled. "He was attacked by a giant fish about six to seven feet long," said the spokeswoman, declining to call it a shark. "The right leg was eaten by the fish. The left leg was wounded."

Lo, 29, was helped to shore by friends and rushed to hospital, but was dead on arrival. He was the second victim in two days, and shark experts think the same shark could be responsible for this and other fatal attacks in the same area this time every year.

On Thursday Tso Kam-Sun, 44, who once represented Hong Kong in swimming at the Asian Games, was found dead in his diving suit off nearby Sai Kung beach with his right leg cleanly severed. Police could not confirm that Tso was killed by a shark.

Australian shark expert Vic Hislop, who came to Hong Kong two years ago after a number of fatal shark attacks, said the shark was a repeat killer and warned of more attacks on the way. "Every year it's been the same," Hislop told government radio. "This time we are awake to it and we've been notified on the 1st of June of the first attack . . . so you've probably got about three weeks that shark will be in your area. Something could be done about it."

The Government recently installed shark-proof nets at a number of key beaches.

The latest attack came as huge crowds came out to the beaches on Friday, a local holiday, many to participate in the annual Dragon Boat races, a traditional festival which celebrates a legendary sea rescue. According to the legend, a minister expelled from high office tried to commit suicide by throwing himself into a river; fishermen had to beat the water furiously with their paddles to prevent him from being eaten by fish.

Reuters World Service, 2 June 1995

CALIFORNIA, USA, 1994

A young woman whose body was found floating off a San Diego beach is believed to have been the victim of a shark attack, lifeguard officials said.

"Large pieces of flesh were missing and we don't know what else could have caused that type of wound," said Lieutenant Brant Bass of the San Diego Lifeguard Service. He said the right leg, most of the left leg and pieces of muscle tissue were missing from the victim's body.

The victim, who was unidentified, is described as white, between eighteen and twenty-four years of age, with brown hair, brown eyes and a butterfly tattoo on her right shoulder. The body was found in an area known as Sunset Cliffs on Friday afternoon by a surfer who had seen a seagull standing on an object in the water and had paddled out to find the mangled corpse.

The area is not generally frequented by swimmers, but its small sandy coves are sometimes used by sunbathers.

Bass said a shark expert called to the scene believed that a great white shark may have attacked the young woman. He said shark attacks were rare in the area, but suggested that those venturing into the waters should be "good swimmers."

Reuters World Service, 16 April 1994

SOUTH CAROLINA, USA, 1994

A woman apparently attacked by a large shark as she swam near Hilton Head Island, South Carolina, was listed in good condition on Monday at Memorial Medical Center in Savannah, where she is being treated for her injuries.

Lioubov Kozarinova, 30, of Gaithersberg, Maryland, was bitten on her right abdomen and left hand during Sunday's attack off North Forest Beach, said her friend and co-worker Alex Grinberg. The two are biologists at the National Institute of Health, who arrived on Saturday to spend a week with friends, he said.

"I was lying on shore and my friend was swimming alone about 200 yards out when the shark attacked," Grinberg said. "She said there was no warning before it hit her like a torpedo." The shark may have been following a shrimp boat working near by, he added.

Kozarinova swam for shore, stunned and unaware at first that she had been bitten, said Grinberg. He and another man rushed into shoulder-deep water and helped the bleeding woman to the beach, where Ralph Wagner, head of the Hilton Head Beach Patrol, radioed for an ambulance and administered first aid.

Wagner said he could not confirm that Kozarinova was attacked by a shark. "I assume it was a fish of some sort, but I've never seen a shark bite," he said, describing Kozarinova's injuries as "severe lacerations."

George H. Burgess, an ichthyologist who directs the International Shark Attack File at the University of Florida in Gainesville, said non-fatal shark attacks are fairly common in Florida, where ten to fifteen occur each year, but are rarer in South Carolina waters. "They have had twenty-two unprovoked attacks, the most recent in 1987, since record-keeping began in the 1800s," he said.

Burgess said five unprovoked attacks, all non-fatal, have been recorded in Georgia waters since 1917. The most recent occurred in the surf of state-owned Jekyll Island in 1962.

Atlanta Journal, 27 September 1994

FLORIDA, USA, 1993

Most parents warn their children about sunburn and the hidden currents when at the beach, but MacIntyre Schaumann's swim turned into an amazing story. He survived a real-life *Jaws* attack—before he was even born.

Cradling her four-month-old baby son to her, Dawn Schaumann says, "MacIntyre William Shark Schaumann is going to be a great surfer one day. And he'll have wild stories to tell his buddies."

The wildest happened in October 1993, before Sharkey, as he is nicknamed, was even born. Dawn, a US champion in the flag-racing—speed—division of lifeguarding, was at her lifeguard station on Treasure Shores Beach, Florida. Even though she was six months pregnant and had earlier hoisted red flags on the beach to warn swimmers of the danger of sharks, the twenty-six-year-old plunged into the sea.

She was only 100 yards out when a surge of pain ripped through her body. "A shark hit me so hard, it felt like a huge truck. The sea turned red around me and my first thought was: my time has come. Then I realised my husband Bill was going to lose me and our baby, all because I'd ignored his warnings of swimming that day. He'd seen bait fish close to the shore, a sign sharks were in the surf. I knew my only chance was to get out of that water pretty fast."

As she had been swimming freestyle, Dawn's left hand had covered her stomach and baby at the moment when the shark attacked. But its top jaw crushed her hand, severing tendons while the bottom jaw bit into her left thigh, close to her femoral artery. Dawn was in incredible pain, but she says, "I swam faster than I'd ever swum before—amazingly, the shark didn't finish us off. I was losing a lot of blood and had to get help."

She rode on a wave and made it ashore, where an elderly couple alerted her lifeguard partner, Chris Henderson. He called an ambulance and her husband Bill, 39, a trained Emergency Medical Technician, who rushed to the beach. He says, "I was the first EMT on the scene and took over the treatment from Chris. I shuddered when I saw the bone-deep bite on Dawn's thigh. Her pulse was weak and her heart was racing out of control."

Finally the ambulance arrived and took her to

hospital. Barely conscious, Dawn told doctors, "I don't want anaesthetic if it's going to harm my baby." After being given painkillers which would not affect the baby, the jagged teeth marks were trimmed and then the thigh wound was closed layer after layer, needing almost 100 stitches.

For weeks it was touch and go for the baby. Dawn went into false labour many times, including an emergency just before Christmas, when she spent ten days in hospital. But, on 15 January, MacIntyre was born three weeks premature, weighing 7 lb. 1 oz. Bill says, "It's a big relief to have such a healthy baby after all he's been through."

Dawn, who is still being treated for damaged hand tendons, adds, "I can't wait to take Sharkey swimming—I don't want him to develop any complexes about the ocean!"

News of the World, London, 29 June 1994

HAWAII, USA, 1991

A Vancouver doctor who was swimming with a friend while on vacation in Hawaii says that she tried to fight off a 4.5-metre Pacific tiger shark with a piece of driftwood minutes before her friend was attacked and killed.

Maui County police Sergeant Waldo Fujie said that Dr. Luise Sourisseau, of West 14th Avenue, Vancouver, and her friend were swimming near Lahaina one morning last week when they noticed a shark which they said was the size of a car swim by.

Sourisseau froze and was brushed by the shark, but her friend Martha Morrell, 41, of Lahaina, was attacked and killed after she panicked and started thrashing around in the water.

"When you splash in the water with any wild animal or predator, they could attack," Fujie said. He added that Sourisseau hit the shark with a piece of driftwood which she saw floating in the water, but was eventually forced to swim to safety while it was attacking Morrell.

The two women had been swimming in front of the Morrells' beach front home. A maid saw the attack and made the initial call to the emergency line.

Fujie said that sharks have been known to frequent that area for feeding during the night. Hawaiian police said that it was the first witnessed shark attack resulting in death in the last thirty-three years. "It is rare for this to happen. You could get into a car accident quicker than a shark attack."

The dead woman's body was recovered with limbs missing. Fujie said one shark was instrumental in the attack, but, since then, there have been reports of at least two or three in the area.

May Sourisseau said her daughter is still in Hawaii with friends, trying to recover from the attack. "It's been very upsetting for her." She added that her daughter, who did not want to be interviewed, said that she had initially thought the shark was a dolphin.

Vancouver Sun, 3 December 1991

HONG KONG, 1991

Eight beaches in the Sai Kung area are expected to remain closed today after an elderly woman was killed yesterday by a shark. The attack, the first of its kind in twelve years, is believed to have been made by a tiger shark.

As a marine patrol launch combed Sai Kung waters yesterday looking for any unusual movement, there were two other reports of alleged shark sightings at the same beach. The gazetted beaches were closed by the Regional Services Department (RSD) after a "large tiger shark" allegedly savaged sixty-five-year-old Yeung Tam-ho while she was swimming off Silverstrand Beach.

Following the death, red flags were hoisted at the eight Sai Kung beaches and signs warning swimmers of shark-infested waters were put up.

The senior fisheries officer with the Agriculture and Fisheries Department, Dr. Paul Mak Mo-shun, believes the attack may have been by a tiger shark more than three metres long. Dr. Mak identified the species after studying photographs of the dead woman at Sai Kung police station.

"Judging from the photos, I cannot think of any other animal that could cause injuries like that," he said. "Her leg was cut off in one bite—it must have been a very big fish."

The woman, who also suffered serious abdominal injuries, disappeared while swimming with a friend outside the restricted area off Silverstrand Beach, near Hung Hau, in Port Shelter. She was a strong swimmer who used the beach regularly, friends said.

A police spokesman said her companion, a thirty-five-year-old man, saw a "large grey fish" swim past him at about 6 am. "He spotted the fish and thought it might be a shark and swam back to shore, but without warning his friend. On the way back to the shore his friend disappeared under the water without making a sound."

The man phoned rescue services and at 7:20 am a Marine Police launch discovered the woman's body. She was certified dead on arrival at United Christian Hospital in Kwun Tong.

South China Morning Post, 9 June 1991

CAPE PROVINCE, SOUTH AFRICA, 1986

A twenty-one-year-old Port Elizabeth student and son of a retired Cape educationist died on the way to George Provincial Hospital after being attacked by a shark near Great Brak River on Sunday. The Outeniqua Divisional Council was investigating the situation urgently to decide whether it will be necessary to close beaches.

Mr. Wessel Olls, a final-year University of Port Elizabeth student, is believed to have been swimming off Eselstrand, between Great Brak River and Glentana Beach, when he was attacked late on Sunday afternoon. He was severely bitten on the left thigh. Some reports said Mr. Olls's leg was bitten off. When asked what happened, his distraught brother, Mr. Anton Olls, said he did not want "to have to go through the whole incident right now."

Mr. Olls was rescued by two lifesavers and given immediate treatment by doctors on the beach.

The superintendent of George Provincial Hospital, Dr. D. M. du Toit, said Mr. Olls was dead when he was brought in at about 6:30 pm. "He had very severe left thigh injuries. The customary police post mortem will be held, but at this stage it is not possible to say what kind of shark it was. The Natal Anti-Shark Measures Board has asked for photographs of the wound to try to establish that."

Mr. Dawie de Vries, secretary of the Outeniqua Divisional Council, said the investigation would first establish precisely where the attack happened before a decision was made on closing beaches. "We can't simply close the beaches to tourists, and I doubt whether panic has set in at this stage. Durban shark authorities said it would be advisable to close the beaches only if the water was murky."

Johannesburg Star, 23 December 1986

FLORIDA, USA, 1981

A man who bet a beer that he could swim three miles to a Gulf Coast island is the second person to die after a shark attack in Florida waters this year, officials say.

Manatee County authorities said Mark Meeker,

26, a Tampa bartender, drowned after a shark took an eight-inch piece out of his right leg.

Six weeks ago, a secretary died off the Atlantic Coast after being attacked by a shark.

Meeker disappeared on Tuesday afternoon after diving off Anna Maria City Pier, three miles across choppy waters and strong tidal currents in the mouth of Tampa Bay. His body was found on Wednesday morning, the drawstring of his bathing suit wrapped tightly around his right thigh as a makeshift tourniquet. Authorities said he drowned after either going into shock or becoming exhausted. Dr Stephen Pelham, Manatee's medical examiner, said that Meeker's wound was the result of a shark attack.

"The marks are consistent with a shark bite," he said. Since sharks have several rows of teeth, a wound left by a shark will generally show other cuts above and below the bite. Meeker's leg had such cuts, he said.

Manatee sheriff's deputy Mark Rominger said Meeker, Meeker's girl friend Angie Tucker and several other friends were on the pier on the south side of Tampa Bay when the bet was made. Rominger said the friends told him they became worried when they lost sight of Meeker after he was just a few hundred yards out. After trying to get a boat to go after him themselves, they alerted the Coast Guard.

On 10 August Christy Wapniarski died after being attacked by a shark while struggling to reach shore a few miles off Daytona Beach.

New Orleans Times-Picayune, 20 September 1981

HONG KONG, 1974

Doctors were last night battling to save the life of an eighteen-year-old boy, a freedom swimmer whose left foot was almost completely torn off by killer sharks.

In a nearby bed at Queen Elizabeth Hospital, his nineteen-year-old friend was being treated for a broken arm and severe lacerations to the body—caused in the same attack. It is believed that a third swimmer in a party of eight, who made their freedom dash from Siu Mui Sha, was killed.

The attack came as the swimmers had almost completed their five-mile crossing to Kai Kung Tau, in Mirs Bay. About 100 yards from the shore at Kai Kung Tau, and with freedom and safety in sight, a pack of sharks slashed into the small group.

The five uninjured swimmers managed to drag the two youths to the shore, where for seven hours they fought to stem the bleeding. Luckily, a police launch arrived. A call went out to Marine Police headquarters, who immediately asked for an RAF helicopter to airlift the injured to hospital. One, with a doctor on board, was sent to Taipo, where it picked up the youths. Ten minutes later they were at the hospital.

The doctor, Flight Lieutenant Chris Ross, said that in most cases all they have to do was give first aid. "But in this case I had to fight for his life."

The two Chinese, Yee Wing-ping and Ho Sin-ming, are believed to be farm workers from the Fa-Yeun Commune near Canton. A Government spokesman said last night that Yee was in a "poor condition"; Ho's condition was "fair." The five uninjured refugees are being held at Marine Police headquarters.

South China Morning Post, 17 August 1974

AMANZIMTOTI, SOUTH AFRICA, 1974

Within seconds of being attacked by a shark in the bathing enclosure of Amanzimtoti yesterday afternoon, a professional lifesaver, Mr. Les Pyper, 33, shouted to two of his colleagues who were swimming close by to clear the bathing area.

The attack took place soon after lunch and scores of bathers saw Mr. Pyper being lifted out of the water as the shark grabbed his leg less than 100 metres from the shore.

Two teenagers, Clive de Witt, 16, and Richard Cuff, 17, who were surfing near by, heard his screams and went to his aid, pulling him to safety on a surfboard. Mr. Pyper received severe lacerations to his right leg and was taken to Addington Hospital with a police escort for emergency treatment.

After hearing Mr. Pyper shout at them to clear the bathing area, one lifesaver, Mr. Brian Fouche, ordered the bathers out of the water, while lifesaver Mr. Derek Fourie ran to their hut and sounded the siren.

A doctor holidaying in the area gave emergency treatment on the beach, while scores of shocked holidaymakers and bathers crowded in, hampering operations. The injured lifesaver was then taken to the hut, where Mr. A. Cloete, a first aid gold medallist from Welkom, stemmed the flow of blood before tourniquets were applied.

Mr. Pyper described later how he fought off the attack by a large lazy grey shark, punching it on the snout while it lifted him out of the water by his right leg. In a hurried interview as he was being pushed to the operating theatre for stitches, he told of the horror when the shark fastened its jaws around his knee.

"I was just swimming along when suddenly I felt the pain. I realized it was a shark and started screaming. I was pretty scared, but managed not to panic. He was very big—I reckon between 400 lbs and 500 lbs. When he lifted me out of the water—that'll give you an idea how big he was—I punched him on the snout. It must have been my lucky day because he let go and swam away, and I screamed to a nearby surfer for help."

Richard Cuff said he was only a few metres from Mr. Pyper when he heard him shout and saw him being lifted out of the water. "He shouted that a shark had attacked him and I saw him struggling in the water."

Clive de Witt said: "I saw a black object beneath the surface and I realized he was not joking. We paddled towards him and helped him on to my board. Blood was streaming from his leg. He had bite marks above and below the knee, and I could see right through to the bone."

Richard Cuff said that, although Mr. Pyper had been bitten, he appeared to be calm, and insisted that the bathers be cleared in a hurry. "He was more worried about the bathers than himself."

An Addington Hospital spokesman last night described Mr. Pyper's condition as "fair."

Cape Times, 8 January 1974

AMANZIMTOTI, SOUTH AFRICA, 1974

A shark savaged two voluntary lifesavers who were swimming in the safe-bathing area at Amanzimtoti last night. This is the second attack at the beach this year. The lifesavers are Joe Kool, 19, and Damon Kendrick, 14, both members of the Amanzimtoti Surf Lifesaving Club.

Damon Kendrick's leg was last night amputated below the knee at Addington Hospital. His condition has been described as "satisfactory." Joe Kool was bitten in the right knee.

"We were all swimming after training on the beach," he said later at the hospital. "I was the farthest out and I felt something hit me in the side. I didn't know what it was. I then felt it grab me in the leg and I hit at whatever I could. It was too dark to see and it let me go.

"I shouted to the others to get back—swim, swim like mad—get back to the shore. I caught a wave to the beach and was running up the beach when I heard Damon shout. I turned round and saw him flung in the air and the blood in the water. I ran back and grabbed him out of the water."

Cape Times, 14 February 1974

DUKE OF YORK ISLANDS, NEW GUINEA, 1966

A school of sharks tore to pieces two young native girls swimming off a reef at the Duke of York Islands, fifteen miles north of Rabaul.

The upper half of one body was the only remains of the two girls which terrified village people recovered after the attack on Sunday.

One of the girls died when she jumped among the sharks in an attempt to rescue her school friend who had been attacked. A third girl tried to jump into the sea, but her father held her back.

The victims were school friends, Memilana Bokset, 13, and Loding Etwat, 9, from Butliwan Village. They were returning from Sunday school with other children and decided to go for a swim off the reef near their homes.

Loding was dragged under the surface by a school of sharks which swam down the edge of the reef. Memilana jumped in to help her, but the girls were torn to pieces in front of the children and adults standing on the reef.

Brisbane Courier Mail, 23 August 1966

NEW SOUTH WALES, AUSTRALIA, 1966

A shark which today mauled a thirteen-year-old boy at Coledale, forty miles south of Sydney, was dragged from the water with its teeth still clamped in the boy's leg. Lifesavers battered the eight-foot shark to death with surfboards as it lay on the beach. The boy is in serious condition in hospital.

The Times, London, 28 February 1966

NATAL, SOUTH AFRICA, 1957

A giant shark attacked and killed Allan Green, a fourteen-year-old Johannesburg schoolboy, while he was swimming less than thirty yards off shore at Uvongo Beach, South Coast, yesterday afternoon.

The tragedy, the second attack on the coast in forty-eight hours, took place in full view of a large crowd of bathers who looked on, horrified, as they heard Allan screaming and saw the shark's tail lashing the water before it pulled him along the surface and then let go. Within minutes bathers formed a human chain and recovered Allan's mutilated body from the blood-stained water.

Mr. John De Gossely, a twenty-year-old Belgian visitor from Johannesburg, said last night that he had been swimming beside Allan just before he was attacked.

"We were about thirty yards off shore. I decided to catch a wave and swim back to the beach. On the way back I heard my father shouting, 'Shark, shark.' He was standing ashore.

"I looked round and saw a black tail lashing the water. It was about two to three feet wide. The shark grabbed Allan and pulled him along the top of the water. He screamed and the water was full of blood. I scrambled on to the beach and some people immediately formed a chain and pulled Allan out of the water. He was already dead and his body was badly mutilated." The right arm and side were torn away.

Mr. De Gossely said that there were about forty people bathing in the small land-locked bay when the shark made its attack. He and Allan had been further out than any of the other bathers.

Allan was on holiday at Uvongo with his parents and his younger brother. They had been staying at the Uvongo Hotel for three weeks and were due to return home on 5 January.

After the tragedy several people reported that they had seen a large shark cruising off shore and Sergeant Stan Cole, station commander of the Margate police, stationed a constable with a rifle on a rock. He stayed there until nightfall, but did not sight the shark.

The attack took place forty-eight hours after another youth, sixteen-year-old Robert Wherley, had his left leg bitten off by a shark at Karridene, about fifty miles from Uvongo [see page 28]. Robert, who lives at Aylesbury Flats, Amanzimtoti, was admitted to the African Explosives Hospital at Umbogintwini. Last night his condition was described as "much improved."

Mr. Frank Shepard, an authority on angling, said last night that there was a danger that the shark might attack again, having tasted human blood. It was quite possible that the same shark was responsible for both attacks. It could easily have swum the distance from Karridene to Uvongo in that time. Judging by the size of the tail which was seen, Mr. Shepard said the shark could have been a "ragged tooth" or a tiger shark. It could weigh between 400 and 500 lbs.

Cape Times, 21 December 1957

NATAL, SOUTH AFRICA, 1957

Four hours after his arrival in Margate yesterday, Vernon James Berry, 23, of Bulawayo [Rhodesia, now Zimbabwe] was taken by a shark and dragged sideways through the surf. He was rescued by two friends, but died on the way to Port Shepstone hospital.

Spectators of the attack, the second fatal one in the last week, said that the young Rhodesian and the shark turned grotesque somersaults in the water. Mr. Berry was taken while he was swimming with a group of more than 200 bathers at a point almost in the centre of the bathing lagoon at Margate. He had arrived in Margate shortly after 1 pm on a five-day visit before going on to motorcycle races in the Cape, where he was to have taken part.

His two companions, Tommy Robinson and Fred Norman, both from Bulawayo, were the first to reach him after the attack and helped him to the beach.

It was thought that the shark had taken him from the side, as Mr. Berry's left forearm was severed, his right arm badly mutilated, his lower abdomen, buttocks and right thigh were also badly mutilated. He was conscious when he was brought back to the beach, but soon lapsed into a coma.

Mr. Robinson said that he was swimming a short distance from Mr. Berry when he heard his cries for help. Someone had also shouted, "Shark!" He did not notice the shark, but saw only his friend floating on his back in a huge streak of blood. As he reached him, he called to their other companion, Fred Norman, who also swam to the mauled man.

They were helped in bringing in Mr. Berry by Mr. D. A. Saunders, of Benoni, who was also swimming near by. Mr. Saunders said that, when Mr. Berry was brought to the beach, he expressed horror at the sight of his own injuries before he lost consciousness. The scene was watched by hundreds of people who thronged the beach at Margate irrespective of the other fatal shark attack, at Uvongo, four miles away, only seventy-two hours before.

Mr. T. J. Erasmus, of Roodepoort, said that he was sitting on the rocks, watching the bathers, when he saw the shark gliding through a breaker to the attack. He shouted, "Shark," but it was too late.

The shark was seen again a few minutes after the attack by Mr. L. Band, of Johannesburg. He said that he saw it quite distinctly as it cruised parallel to the beach. At one point he could see its entire length as it swam along a breaking wave. He estimated its length to be more than ten feet.

The shark was first seen swimming past a group of Native bathers to the north of the main Margate beach. One of the Natives ran to the European beach to warn the lifesavers, but was beaten by the fast-swimming shark.

The Margate surf was deserted for the rest of the afternoon.

Cape Times, 24 December 1957

VICTORIA, AUSTRALIA, 1956

A shark killed a twenty-seven-year-old lifesaver at Portsea, at the entrance of Port Phillip Bay, this afternoon.

The victim was John Patrick Wishart, a plumber, of Sorrento. His wife and seventeen-year-old sister were on the beach at the time.

Wishart was not seen again after the shark took him. The shark attacked while the lifesaver and five friends were swimming about 250 yards from the crowded beach.

Gregory Warland, 20, a sergeant in the College of Officer Cadets at Portsea, said after the attack, "Wishart was near me in the water, about five yards away. Hopper (a friend) was between us. Suddenly a shark about twelve feet long swam past Hopper. It hit him in the stomach with its tail, then swam towards Wishart.

"Suddenly there was a splash, and I could see the

snout and the jaws of the shark above the surface of the water. Then it seemed to splash down on top of Wishart. It was about four yards away. There was a swirl in the water—and then nothing.

"Hopper and I tried to find Wishart. We realised it was useless, and swam madly for the shore. I reached the shore first and rushed up to the club house to see if I could see anything from there. Then I ran back to help Hopper ashore. I was so shocked I didn't even tell anybody at first. In the meantime the other three chaps had swum ashore."

Mrs. G. Bell, of Aspendale, who saw the attack, said, "Suddenly one of the men threw up his arms and went under. We thought he was just playing about in the water, but then he began to thrash his arms about and we realized he was being attacked. Then we saw the shark's fin. The man struggled and seemed to be punching the shark, but then his struggles weakened and he disappeared."

Lifesavers tonight patrolled the beach in the hope of finding Wishart's body.

Sydney Morning Herald, 5 March 1956

YEMEN (FORMERLY ADEN), 1955

Aden fisherman Mohammed Arecki..., armed with only an iron rod, replied to the screams of a woman swimmer [Mrs. W. F. Dixon, wife of Wing Commander Dixon] being attacked by an eight-foot-long shark in Telegraph Bay, Aden.

The shark severed part of an arm and a leg, and

ripped a gaping hole in the woman's back. With his arm round the victim, the fisherman fought off the shark with such determination that it was forced to release her mutilated body . . .

The maddened fish then turned on the fisherman, jaws snapping, and tried to cause him to let go of its intended victim. Mohammed Arecki succeeded in struggling ashore with the woman and gave her first aid until an ambulance arrived. [Mrs. Dixon subsequently died of her injuries.]

Baltimore Evening Sun, 27 September 1955

BERMUDA, 1954

Sub-Lieutenant E. M. Marks, aged twenty-two, who is serving with HMS *Sheffield*, was flown to London yesterday from Bermuda for emergency treatment for injuries received when a shark attacked him while bathing.

The condition of Sub-Lieutenant E. M. Marks, who was flown to London from Bermuda for emergency treatment after being attacked by a shark while bathing, is stated by Chatham Naval Hospital to be "quite satisfactory."

The Times, London, 10 and 12 July 1954

QUEENSLAND, AUSTRALIA, 1951

The first shark casualty on the Queensland beaches
this summer occurred on Saturday 20 October at
Townsville, north Queensland, when a shark
evaded the protective wire netting and fatally injured a swimmer.

The Times, London, 23 October 1951

SOUTH AUSTRALIA, AUSTRALIA, 1940

Maxwell Arthur Farrin, 13, of Jacobson Avenue,
Brighton, was killed by a shark while he was swimming about fifty yards from the shore at North
Brighton yesterday morning. His left leg was severed and he suffered other injuries.

Although the shark, which is believed to be of the
tiger species, remained in the vicinity, Mr. Sydney
Owen, 48, dashed into the sea and brought the boy
ashore. The boy died almost immediately afterwards.

The last fatal shark attack on metropolitan
beaches occurred when David Paton was taken at
South Steyne in September 1936.

Farrin went to the beach opposite Bestic Street
with Kenneth Moore, 12, also of Jacobson Avenue,

and Harry Flower, 11, a cousin of Moore, of Melford Street, Hurlstone Park.

"We were paddling about on the edge of the beach while Max swam out about fifty yards," said Moore. "The sea was very calm. We heard a noise like a groan, and saw Max lying face downwards with blood all round him. We called to him, but he didn't answer."

"When a boy ran to me and said that another boy was covered in blood in the water, I ran into the sea," said Mr. Robert Ambrose, of Frederick Street, St. Peters. "I saw the fin of a large shark close to him and I ran over the sandhill to General Holmes Drive, where I stopped a lorry to get a length of rope to try and pull the boy in."

Mr. Owen, whose home in General Holmes Drive faces the spot where Farrin had been swimming, said he heard shouts that a boy had been attacked by a shark. "I was watering my garden," he said, "but I dropped the hose, and in my shorts and a shirt I raced over the sandbank. I saw Farrin floating face downward, and, as I waded out towards him, someone on the beach shouted that the shark was still there.

"I waded out and splashed about until the sea was beyond my depth. Then I swam to the boy, who was floating in about twelve feet of water. When I caught hold of him, I could see that he had been shockingly injured.

"The shark was then not more than ten feet away. It seemed to be at least ten feet long. Luckily, it did not attack again. When I reached shallow water, others helped me carry the boy on to the sand."

The mother of the boy, who had rushed to the

beach, collapsed as her son was brought ashore. The St. George Ambulance wrapped the boy in blankets and rushed him to the St. George Hospital, but he was then dead. His injuries, apart from the loss of his leg, were so severe that doctors expressed the opinion that he died as Mr. Owen laid him on the beach.

The boy and his sister were the only children in the Farrin family. The boy attended the Hurstville Technical School and he showed great promise as a commercial artist. He had spent most of his school holidays drawing aeroplanes and motor cars for his school friends, and after his death yesterday they collected all his drawings and put them away for safe keeping. Farrin had won a lifesaving certificate . . .

Mr. W. A. Jackson, health inspector of the Rockdale Council, said that he saw the shark swimming about the spot where the boy was attacked for some time afterwards. "It is too risky for children to swim in the open sea as the bay is infested with sharks," he said. "While no swimmer has lost his life previously from a shark attack along the foreshore, the sharks frequently tear the nets of fishermen, and they snap at fishing baits. The Rockdale Council provides an enclosed bath where swimming is safe and children are admitted for a penny."

Sydney Morning Herald, 24 January 1940

QUEENSLAND, AUSTRALIA, 1934

Roy Inman, 14, of Wordsworth Avenue, Concord, was taken by a shark at Horsefield Bay, Brisbane Water, about a mile from Woy Woy, before the eyes of his mother and two sisters yesterday afternoon.

The water was lashed to foam as the shark seized the boy, whose head appeared once above the surface. Then the shark returned to the attack and Inman was dragged beneath the water. His body has not been recovered.

The boy's twelve-year-old sister, Joyce, had a narrow escape. The shark brushed against her as it sped through the water, its fin wounding one of her legs.

The tragedy occurred a few seconds after the boy dived from a short jetty in front of the cottage in which he was staying. His older sister, Kathleen, 26, was standing at the door of the cottage, watching the children, and she saw the terrible tragedy. She made gallant attempts to rescue her brother after the initial attack, but reached the scene in a rowing boat too late to render him any assistance.

Throughout yesterday the boy and his two sisters, accompanied by others from nearby houses, had been swimming in the water and diving either from the front of the house or the jetty into the water, which is about ten feet deep. Shortly after lunch the Inman children decided to return to the water. Joyce and Roy arrived at the end of the jetty a few minutes before their elder sister, who changed into her swimming costume, intending to follow them immediately. While they were awaiting her arrival, they decided to hold a diving competition. Joyce dived from the jetty into the water. Roy applauded her effort, but said he could make less splash, and he plunged into the bay.

Just as he struck the water, Joyce screamed with terror. A huge black fin cut through the water towards her. She saw the shark when it was a few feet away. The shark apparently misjudged the location of its intended victim, for, as she kicked out, she felt it graze her leg and felt a sharp stinging pain in her calf. Then she saw her brother disappear in a swirl of foam, and she swam for the jetty a few feet away.

Mrs. Inman was sitting on the verandah at the time and saw her son taken. She screamed out, "Shark," and saw Roy seized.

While the two children were diving, Kathleen arrived at the door of the house and stood watching them plunge into the water about twenty feet from her. Then she saw the shark racing towards the children. An instant later the boy's scream rang out, and the head of her brother was dragged down. With a cry of alarm, she ran to where a rowing boat was moored. She jumped into it and pushed off with an oar. She had almost reached her brother when the shark returned and, despite the struggles of the boy, dragged him down. Kathleen frantically searched the locality, pushing the oar down into the water in the hope that it would touch the shark and make it release its victim.

"Roy was seized by the monster and it dragged him down," Kathleen Inman said in telling the story of the tragedy. "Before I reached him the shark had grabbed him again and pulled him below the water. It was terrible. The boat was right over the shark and it was just covered with blood. It disappeared. I did not see it again. Other boats came over, but we could not find him."

In the meantime, Mr. Inman arrived and the search was continued. Kathleen was taken ashore. Immediately she rushed to the house occupied by the Wasson family next door, and warned them against allowing their children to swim in the bay. Later in the evening the Inmans returned to their home in Sydney.

During the afternoon the police at Woy Woy, which is about a mile from the bay, were notified of the tragedy, and Constable McKenzie hurried to the cottage. Sergeant Ravelli and a constable from the Newcastle Water Police joined McKenzie later, and they commenced dragging for the body. Their efforts had been unsuccessful when the search was abandoned at about eight o'clock.

For some weeks sharks have been seen in the bay and a warning had been issued to holidaymakers against bathing there. Local fishermen had spent considerable time in trying to catch the monsters.

Roy Inman was one of the most popular boys at the Concord public school. He was a diligent pupil. He took a keen interest in sport and was one of the best swimmers in the school.

Sydney Morning Herald, 24 December 1934

SOUTH AUSTRALIA, AUSTRALIA, 1930

Attacked by a shark off the end of the Middle Brighton Pier yesterday afternoon, Norman William Clark, aged nineteen years, of North Brighton, was mutilated and dragged to his death before assistance could be obtained.

Between 80 and 100 people saw Clark disappear. So sudden was the attack that few people realised what had happened until they saw the shark grip Clark in its jaws. It attacked him again and again, and eventually disappeared with the body fifty feet from the shore. Witnesses said that the shark was at least sixteen feet long.

Clark was treading water when the shark first attacked him. Suddenly he cried out and, throwing up one hand, disappeared under the surface. When he came up, the shark could be seen holding on to his leg. Clark appeared to be sitting across its nose and was punching it with his hands. Several women on the pier, including a girl in whose company Clark had been, fainted. Others tried to frighten the shark away with noise. It again disappeared and dragged Clark to the other side of the pier. When the youth came up again, he was still trying to beat off the shark, but his strength was fast ebbing.

The shark let him go, and then, with its fin and tail out of the water, made another rush at him. It almost lifted him from the water as it seized him around the chest in its jaws.

That was the last seen of Clark, who was dragged under by the shark and apparently carried away.

Experienced fishermen at Brighton claim that they have been warning people for weeks that there were sharks around the pier.

Sydney Morning Herald, 17 February 1930

UK, AUSTRALIA AND ADEN (NOW YEMEN), 1906

Letters to the Editor of *The Times*, London

Sir—Eight years ago, writing from this port [Mevagissey, Cornwall], I ventured to warn those who bathe from yachts and small boats anywhere within the ten-mile limit against the risk of an encounter with the blue or porbeagle sharks well known to swim no further from the Cornish coast on hot summer days. Only four days ago some of the local mackerel crews saw a blue shark, seven or eight feet long, swimming within Chapel Point—that is to say, not more than a mile from the harbour. A little further back a large party of visitors were fishing for pollack five or six miles off. A brand new line was then essayed, with the result that the monster was finally captured. Its measurements were, I regret to say, not taken, but some idea may be formed of its weight when I mention that five men were unable to drag it with the aid of a rope from the quay to their lodgings not far distant.

Fresh as I am from the Florida shores of the Gulf of Mexico, where on one occasion I had the misfortune to hook a leopard shark fourteen feet long, these Cornish marauders seem very puny; but they might, for all that, prove unpleasant bathing companions at close quarters. It has admittedly never been demonstrated that they will attack a swimmer in daylight; on the other hand, it has yet to be proved that they will not; and it is against involuntary settling of this vexed question that I once more make bold to warn your readers.

The coves along this coast, in which the water is deep enough for diving and clear enough to satisfy the most fastidious, are too many and too beautiful for there to be the need of this foolhardy practice of bathing from yachts' dinghies outside the headlands. On the other hand, these large sharks afford most exciting sport, being the only really big game in our seas, and a tussle with one is always an attraction—at the further end of a line. Anyone who sounds such a warning at that conveyed in this letter runs the risk of being abused as a sensationmonger, but I imagine that most would be willing to take that risk in the hope of averting possible disaster.

Your obedient servant,

Mevagissey, 3 August 1906   F. G. Aflalo

Sir—The warning to bathers published in *The Times* recently is a repetition of history. Even a caution from the same source which appeared eight years ago was by no means the first of its kind, for as far back as the year 1876 another, dated from Hastings, was circulated in the London Press.

The presence of sharks in British seas, contested even today by ill-informed persons, is appreciated only by those who fish for either sport or their livelihood as a very real evil. The larger sharks, of the blue and porbeagle kinds, make their presence felt inshore only in the hottest July and August weather . . .

It is, however, with the two summer kinds that the bather is chiefly concerned, since not only is salt-water bathing confined for the most part to the summer months, but it is only in a high temperature that, mindful perhaps of their centre of distribution in tropical seas, these tyrants venture to attack man. The greatest of all sharks, the huge basking shark or sail-fish, which yachtsmen occasionally encounter off the Irish coast and even near the Land's End, is a perfectly harmless creature, feeding on entomostraca, and incapable of attacking even the feeblest human being. To this species, no doubt, belonged an example measuring thirty feet in length which was found entangled in seventeen nets at Hastings in the year 1810. It was purchased by Colonel Bothwell "for his friend Mr. Home, the surgeon of Sackville Street, who intends to dissect it and place the skeleton in his museum." It is believed by some that this is the skeleton in the Natural History Museum, London.

Of bathers being seized by sharks on the British coast there is, it is true, no record. At the same time it is well to remember that it is exceedingly improbable that there would be. Sharks are notorious cowards . . . Sharks, unless encouraged by numbers of their own kind or by the helplessness of a solitary swimmer, give man a wide berth. It is, therefore, only the lonely bather who has anything to fear from these cowardly animals, and bathing, at any rate along our coasts in summer time, is a gregarious exercise. One swimmer among many would run little or no risk.

One of the well-known diving boys at Aden, whose evolutions round anchored liners have recently been discontinued by order of the authorities, contrived for many years to attract much sympathy and baksheesh by the loss of one of his legs, reputedly by a shark bite. The present writer interrogated him on the subject many years ago, and from him had a circumstantial account of his adventure. It has, however, since transpired, possibly when the prohibition of diving put an end to the profits from this source, that his leg was taken off by the screw of a steamer, from which he was not able to get clear, and thus one of the few authentic cases of sharks attacking human beings disappears from the list.

A very small boy in the company of others was badly bitten by a shark in Sydney Harbour in the winter (Australian) of 1895, but the case was exceptional. The lad's cap had blown out into deeper water, out of the "white water" range to which Sydney swimmers are careful to keep, and it was in floundering after it that he met with his accident, which was said to have resulted in death the same night from hemorrhage.

So far, it must be admitted, the evidence of death from sharks in English seas is altogether negative, but it is an article of firm belief with many well acquainted with the ways of these creatures that many of the cases of drowning from alleged cramp, in which the victim disappears and the body is never found, are in reality cases of seizure, not by cramp, but by sharks. Obviously, the theory is a matter of opinion only and cannot be argued to a logical conclusion.

A very interesting and in many ways unique experience lately came under the writer's notice, in which, in the year 1876, a gentleman, who plainly remembers every detail and has the evidence of a long letter written to a relative at the time, was almost certainly as near death from this cause as any one could be and yet escape.

He was bathing alone from the beach between Hastings and Fairlight [Sussex, England], and had swum out to an anchored smack about 400 yards from the shore. Returning almost immediately, he was carried sideways by a strong ebb tide and, when about 100 yards from the smack, he felt something in contact with his left leg. He struck out wildly, and immediately his left arm rubbed along some kind of fish. At this he shouted and swam with all his might, and two or three times more the fish scraped alongside him, but he managed to attract the attention of two men in a small boat, and into this he almost vaulted in his anxiety to get out of such company. A large fish was seen swimming round the boat, undoubtedly a blue or porbeagle shark, and the fishermen of the district were unanimously of the opinion that it had been a very near thing.

Why, it may be asked, did the shark not seize him and have done with it? Those who have had much traffic with sharks will at once recognize in the episode their invariable behaviour with any kind of bait. They always swim round it half a dozen times, nosing it, rubbing their body against it, and then, if all is well, they seize it in their teeth. All was not well on the occasion referred to, for the bait behaved most uncommonly, throwing out its arms and legs, and shouting at the top of its voice, a performance more than enough to scare any shark in comparatively shallow water.

The recent warning, then, touching the foolishness of bathing at any considerable distance from the shore in summer weather might have been coupled with a rider indicating the yet greater risk of bathing alone. In company with others, who might, and probably would, make a great deal of noise and commotion in the water, the risk would be slight. On the other hand, a solitary swimmer, too faint-hearted to frighten off his pursuer, would almost certainly go under, first with cramp induced by the paralysis of fear, and then with the shark's teeth in his body. This would never be recovered, and there would be one more disappearance, with perhaps its sequel in the Probate Court some years later.

20 August 1906   From a Correspondent

Sir—In a long communication in your issue of yesterday your Correspondent takes up the cudgels on behalf of the shark as an innocent and harmless bathing companion. The most serious impropriety which he will impute to the shark is that occasionally, like the tiger in the children's rhyme, "he comes and snaggles with his nose." He dismisses as apocryphal all the stories of bathers seized by sharks, and on the strength of one of the Aden diving boys having had his leg taken off by a ship's propeller and not by a shark, he remarks, "thus one of the few authentic cases of sharks attacking human beings disappears from the list."

Now I am afraid that this is a case of protesting

too much. I happened to be on board a vessel off Aden when one of those cases occurred. I did not see the shark, but I saw the boy dive and reappear almost immediately with his leg bitten off above the knee. My recollection is very distinct that the propeller was at rest at the time. Moreover, judging from the place where the boy dived and the short time he was below water, it would have been necessary for the propeller, in order to reach him, to have left its place at the stern, to have rushed with ferocious speed to a point more than half the length of the vessel and some distance out from the ship's side, and to have afterwards returned to its proper position and have fixed itself there without exciting notice.

I am afraid I must continue to believe, in spite of your Correspondent, that that boy's leg at any rate was bitten off. On another occasion I was cabin mate for some time with a man who had recently been for some days hanging in the rigging of a vessel wrecked in tropical waters, and his knowledge of sharks and their ways was, like Mr. Weller's knowledge of London, extensive and peculiar.

But, while I respectfully question your Correspondent's premises, I fully endorse his conclusions, and for the future shall forsake the seclusion of the solitary swimmer for the vulgar security of mixed bathing.

I am yours faithfully,
Seal, Sevenoaks, 21 August 1906 H. Whitbread

5
Surfing the Waves

It was a glorious hot Saturday and the rollers were good. Andrew Carter, one of South Africa's top professional surfers, was lying face down on his board, paddling hard, some 200 yards off East London's Indian Ocean shore, when he was hit from nowhere by the most powerful force he had felt in his thirty-one-year life.

Pinned to his surfboard, he twisted his neck and looked over his left shoulder. "I saw a big, black shiny head," he said. "Its teeth were embedded in my thigh and my board. We were gripped in its mouth like a big sandwich."

The mouth belonged to a great white shark, the marine beast of *Jaws* fame. Despite the horror of last month's attack, Carter survived, with terrible wounds to his buttock and thigh, which needed 400 stitches.

He was lucky: his friend and fellow surfing freak, twenty-two-year-old Bruce Corby, was attacked by the same shark and died. A third surfer, John Borne, was near both Carter and Corby as the great white first struck.

When Borne saw Carter in the jaws of the shark, he began paddling through the reddened sea towards him. As the shark released its grip to take another bite, Carter rolled off the board—just in time, because the shark clamped its jaws on the board and took a huge chunk out of it. As the great white dived, Carter grabbed the board again and caught a tow from a wave. Borne joined him on the same wave, and they were carried on to the shore.

"I began hollering, 'Shark attack,' " said Borne, "Then I saw Bruce [Corby] coming in and asked him if he had seen what happened. His words to me were, 'John, I've just lost my leg.' "

When Bruce Corby got to the shore, they could see the extent of his injuries. His right leg had been severed at the knee by the great white. His injury was severe, though survivable—but soon afterwards he stopped breathing. Fellow surfers pumped his lungs and tied an emergency tourniquet. But Corby never regained full consciousness and died in hospital several hours later.

Corby was the first person to die from a great white attack in South Africa since the country took steps three years ago to protect the shark from their only predator—man. Anyone who kills a great white in South African waters faces a fine of £10,000 or six years' imprisonment. Neither Corby's death nor Carter's injuries are doing much to slow the march of the great white fan club. Shark expert Craig Ferreira plans to visit Britain next month [August 1994], for instance, to canvass support for great white conservation.

"You can't talk about 'man-eating' white sharks," said Ferreira, who is field officer of Cape Town's White Shark Research Project (WSRP), "White shark attacks on humans are very rare and, when it happens, there's nothing personal about it. It's just doing what nature designed it for and, if you go surfing or diving, you have to accept that you're invading its space."

He will try to persuade diving clubs around Britain to visit South Africa for practical courses on the shark. At the same time, he hopes to persuade groups of enthusiasts and businesses to adopt individual great whites at £1,000 a time—a scheme already successful in Sweden to help finance the work of the WRSP. The project was launched in 1990 by Craig's father, Theo Ferreira, who was once the most renowned white shark hunter in southern Africa. He turned conservationist several years ago, when a fifteen-foot monster he had caught and towed into harbour refused to die despite being stabbed through the gill plates six times and having five bullets pumped into it.

"I realised for the first time, after mutilating it until the whole sea turned red, that we were dealing with a magnificent creature with a mighty will to live. I felt embarrassment and remorse, and I haven't hunted the great white since."

Craig and Theo now spend many weeks of each year on the waves helping research into great whites by tagging them so that individual animals can be tracked.

"No two white sharks ever behave in the same way," said Theo. "You can get very attached to a particular creature. We pat some of them on their heads like big puppy dogs. But you must be aware all the time that you're dealing with the King of the Heap who can destroy your life in one foul blow."

White sharks are extremely rare with only up to 1,200 around South Africa's 1,850-mile coastline. The conservation laws were introduced when scientists realized there were very few breeding adults left—as a result of big-game anglers taking trophy fish whose jaws sell for substantial amounts on the American market.

"In four or five years this legislation will ensure that our great white numbers begin recovering," said Theo Ferreira. "Meanwhile, I'm getting great pleasure and satisfaction in helping counteract shark abuse. You can't wipe out a species just because it occasionally comes in contact with humans."

Andrew Carter, reflecting on his lucky escape, reluctantly agrees. "It would be senseless to go on a hunting spree for that thing, as many people in East London wanted to do. But I obviously feel hostile and angry towards that particular shark. It killed my friend and, whatever the Ferreiras say, they haven't proved that a great white might not get a taste for man."

Sunday Telegraph, London, 31 July 1994

When it comes to killer sharks Andrew Carter is probably the world's leading human guinea pig. He is the only man to have survived a double attack by a great white shark, which left him seconds from death. In the horrific encounter off the coast of South Africa, Andrew's right leg was bitten to the bone from hip to knee. His best friend died from massive injuries inflicted by the same shark.

The attack was twelve months ago, but in the next month Andrew will attempt to overcome his fear by returning to surf in the same waters in which he was attacked.

The memories of what happened are still vivid. "There was a fabulous clear blue sky and I'd been out surfing for about half an hour with my friend Bruce Corby," he remembers. "Suddenly, I felt this huge bang from behind. I realized straight away it was a shark. The first three seconds were the worst, sheer terror like I could never have imagined.

"I remember its power. It was the most helpless feeling because it had its jaws clamped round my leg and my surfboard, pulling me down into the water. I felt like my bones were being crushed. Its jaws alone were about four or five feet long. I looked down into its face. I think its eyes were probably closed.

"I could feel it was biting me, but I didn't feel much pain because my adrenalin was racing. It was just a crushing sensation and fear of dying because I was so far off shore, about 200 metres, where you're totally helpless, in the shark's domain.

"The guy who was closest to me said I let out one piercing scream. He said he thought the shark was biting me in half because its jaw was right over my leg, and the water all around me just flowed red. He turned round and paddled for dear life and I can understand why. You can't help someone escape from a shark that size."

Carter thought that he was being eaten alive. "It

was a feeling of such unbelievable horror. I was holding on to my surfboard with all my might. Then for some reason the shark opened its mouth, probably to get a bigger bite. It went back into the water and leapt forward again. Because I was holding my board so tight, it twisted round and jammed in the shark's mouth, and I started to swim a few strokes away.

"I kept looking back because I was terrified it would come at me from behind. And then I saw it let go of the board and disappear. I knew then that it was coming after me.

"I was too far from shore and losing an enormous amount of blood, so I knew I was minutes away from passing out. In desperation I clawed my way back to my surfboard and, as I grabbed it, I caught the luckiest wave of my life, which carried me in to shore."

He saw two girls sunbathing on the beach and started shouting for help. One girl tore off her clothes, tied them round his leg and packed them into the massive wound.

"She was holding my hand all the time. I was very cold and could feel the warmth from her body flowing into me. It was then that I thought I would die and started to see my life flowing past my eyes. My vision went, I could barely hear, but I realized I had no fear of death and was completely at ease with myself."

Andrew's friend, Bruce, was further out and had to come through Carter's blood to escape. None of the witnesses realized he was the shark's second victim until they saw him dying.

"A guy on the beach saw Bruce coming in on a

wave," Carter says. "He shouted, 'Get out of the water. Andrew's been attacked.' Bruce said, 'I've been attacked too,' but apparently he seemed very normal. Only then did the guy look down at him and see that he didn't have a leg. He grabbed Bruce and pulled him out of the water, and Bruce became totally hysterical. He went into shock and within about two minutes he'd stopped breathing. They gave him artificial respiration on the beach and revived him, but he was brain dead from that moment on and died forty-eight hours later."

Carter had a five-hour operation involving around 2,000 stitches. Every muscle and tendon had to be painstakingly sewed back together.

The champion surfer, who has won South African and European titles, remembers that only about two inches of flesh held his leg on to his torso. "The attack changed me a great deal," he says now. "It was a big thing to realize I have no fear of death when it comes to it. I used to get very uptight waiting for people when they were late or hanging about for a plane, whereas now I sit back and relax. I feel as though I'm living on borrowed time . . .

"Now I have to go back to the place I was attacked to overcome my fear forever. I've been surfing for twenty-two years and only been attacked once. If anything, I think I'm kind of invincible now because I can get away from the buggers."

Independent, London, 29 September 1995

CALIFORNIA, USA, 1995

A Santa Cruz windsurfer escaped injury when he was attacked by a shark just off Davenport Landing on Friday.

The surfer involved in the 5:30 pm attack just north of Davenport, identified as Mike Sullivan, could not be reached for comment on Saturday, but Matt Haut, who works at Haut Surf and Sail in Santa Cruz, said he witnessed the incident, which he termed "pretty hairy."

"I saw this real thrashing, lots of white water spray everywhere," said Haut, who was windsurfing thirty or forty feet from the spot of the attack. "I saw his board being carried upwind and I saw him swimming frantically away from his gear. I knew something was wrong and I sailed up between him and his board. I saw death in his eyes, he was really, really scared."

Although the attacked surfer managed to swim ashore and was not hurt, Haut said, his board was pocked with teeth marks. Ben Christi, who also witnessed the accident, said, "There were teeth marks on both rails of the board, on one side between his rear and front straps, and on the other side near the fin—a span of maybe two feet—that's the mouth span."

"It's definitely a shark bite," said Sean Van Sommeran, executive director of the Pelagic Shark Research Foundation in Santa Cruz, who examined the bitten board and talked with several witnesses. He estimated the animal's size at twelve to sixteen feet.

San Jose Mercury News, 10 January 1995

RECIFE, BRAZIL, 1995

A dramatic increase in shark attacks is threatening local surfers and the economy in Recife, a popular resort in north-east Brazil. Despite a ban on surfing, a shark claimed another life last month. International shark experts will meet in Brazil in November to study the problem.

Local surfers and fishermen say they cannot remember any shark attacks off the palm-fringed beaches of Recife before 1992. Then, suddenly, they started. In 1994 alone, there were eleven attacks along a ten-kilometre stretch of coast. The sharks go mainly for surfers, though three swimmers have also been attacked, all of them outside the coral reef which shelters most of the beaches.

Researchers believe that surfers are more susceptible to shark attacks because of the movements they make on the surface of the water while waiting for waves, and because they spend more time in deep water.

The first response of the local government was to put up signs in Portuguese and English which said: "Surfers, be cool! Respect natural boundaries. Do not go beyond the reef." But the signs neglected to mention sharks. Local oceanographer Favio Hazin accused the government of "hiding its head in the sand." Locals began spray-painting sharks on to the signs, and surfers held a protest on the beach, complete with a bloody, mauled mannequin.

When the new state government came into power in January [1995], it promptly banned surfing and bolstered Hazin's shark research efforts at the Federal Rural University of Pernambuco. Since the crisis began, Hazin's team have caught more than 200 sharks in order to study their behaviour and life cycle. The shark meat is donated to feed hungry local children. Meanwhile, police have begun patrolling the beaches, confiscating boards from surfers who defy the ban.

"What is happening in many areas of the world is that aquatic recreation is beginning to take off, and so shark attacks are more frequent," says George Burgess, director of the International Shark Attack File at the University of Florida in Gainesville, USA. The recent spate of shark attacks off popular beaches in Hong Kong [see chapters 1 and 4] supports this view. However, Brazilian surfers have been holding championships off the beaches near Recife since the 1970s, so the increase in surfing cannot entirely explain the sudden surge of shark attacks.

In a preliminary unpublished report, Hazin and his colleagues point an accusing finger at the port of Suape, built in 1989 just south of the three beaches where most of the attacks have occurred. The port may be bringing people and sharks into closer contact, they say. The researchers found a correlation between months when there are more passing ships, and months when there are shark attacks. Sharks are known to follow big ships, especially if sailors are dumping rubbish overboard. Hazin's team has found an onion, a pineapple and a can of beer in the stomachs of local sharks.

From the imprint in a bite-shaped piece of styrofoam body-board, the biologists have identified one of the culprits as a bull shark, although there is also evidence that tiger sharks are responsible for some attacks.

The Brazilians are now seeking advice on whether to install safety nets around the beaches of Recife . . . Educating local surfers to avoid going out at dawn and dusk, when the sharks are most active, to avoid water where there are birds diving and fish jumping, and to avoid channels where sharks tend to congregate may all help.

This type of advice, however, may simply be water off a surfer's back. "Those surfers who get bitten by sharks here wear their scars as a badge of honour," says Burgess. "The more dangerous they think it is, the more attractive surfing is for some people," says Hazin. "I try to emphasize that they're not only risking their lives, they're damaging the state economy."
New Scientist, 19 August 1995

FLORIDA, USA, 1995

Briton James Oatley was savaged in a shark attack while on holiday in Florida.

The twenty-year-old mechanic had been surfing at Daytona Beach when the *Jaws*-style beast struck.

It grabbed his upper thigh and pushed him out of the water as he waded through the shallows. Unsure what had happened, James struggled to the shore with blood pouring from his wounds.

When he finally managed to examine his injuries, he was horrified to find two long rows of teeth marks along his leg. A friend managed to pull him further up the shore before the shark could strike again. James is the summer's ninth victim of shark attacks along the Daytona stretch of the Atlantic coastline.

After receiving treatment for his wounds, he said: "I felt a tug like a dog biting me—it was pretty scary. I've been shark fishing before—now they are fighting back. But this will not stop me going surfing or to the beach."

His shocked parents said he had been lucky to escape with his life. Speaking at the family home in South Warnborough, Alton, Hants, his mum Christine said: "James was taken to hospital and had lots of antibiotics and a tetanus injection. Fortunately, he is not going to lose his leg. He will be flying home at the weekend, but he'll be in a wheelchair because he can't walk."

James's relieved dad George joked: "I'm going to buy him a *Jaws* poster for his room when he gets back." The couple last saw their son about ten weeks ago when he flew off to Florida for an extended holiday.

Beach authorities in the area estimated the shark was about six feet long—slightly bigger than the beasts blamed for similar attacks this year. Experts say sharks looking for small fish are mistakenly attracted to the thrashing and bright colours of surfers and swimmers. Last month four surfers were bitten on the same beach, one receiving stitches on a four-inch gash. And ten days ago, Matt Sturgess, 12, was bitten on the leg while surfing.

London Daily Star, 18 August 1995

HOOKIPA, 1993

When Scott Shoemaker was attacked at Hookipa, the shark's motivation was probably territorial rather than a hankering for a tasty meal. Shoemaker was sailing at full speed, well away from the shore, when a sudden impact caused his board to spin out, leaving him dangling from his boom with a four- to five-foot reef shark attached to one thigh.

He let go of the boom, pushed the shark off with his hand and crawled on to his board to await the next attack. When none came, he mustered his nerve, jumped in the water, rearranged his rig, water-started and sailed to shore. His friends whisked him off to hospital.

Shoemaker says he felt no pain, but the look of terror in his eyes must have been quite a sight.

Windsurfing, September/October 1993

HAWAII, USA, 1992

It was little more than a year ago when Rick Gruzinsky, a construction worker from suburban Honolulu, was sitting on his surfboard at dawn at an offshore reef near Laniakea on Oahu's north shore. His friend had caught a small wave in. Gruzinsky was alone.

Or so he thought.

Lurking near by in the blue-green sea was a fourteen-foot tiger shark. It swirled beneath Gruzinsky, then crashed the surface and clamped down on the front of his surfboard, shaking its head and snapping off a large chunk. Gruzinsky vividly remembers seeing the chunk stuck in the shark's open mouth as the startled surfer climbed back on to his broken board and raced back to shore.

Reached the other day at his home in Hawaii Kai, Gruzinsky, 28, said he has not quit surfing, but he cannot shake the memory of that attack on 22 October 1992. Nor can anyone else in and even beyond the surfing community on Oahu.

Gruzinsky's was only the first of three confirmed attacks within a period of two months, including the fatal attack at Keaau Beach Park on bodyboarder Aaron Romento, who bled to death after being bitten on the leg shortly after reaching shore screaming for help.

And then there was Gary Chun, who, like Gruzinsky, saw his board snatched and bitten by a large shark while Chun was waiting for a wave near Laniakea. He escaped with minor injuries.

Subsequent sightings and alleged sightings were reported by the dozens last winter as the situation bordered on hysteria, prompting a shark scare of unprecedented proportions and the first comprehensive shark hunts since the early 1970s . . .

"According to my records, fifty-eight large tiger

sharks were taken around Oahu, so I think we may have made a substantial dent in the population," said John Naughton, a National Marine Fisheries Service biologist and prominent member of the recently disbanded state shark task force. "Obviously there are still some around—but one thing, it seems to have really reduced the number of attacks around Oahu . . ."

Some good [seems] to have come of the attacks and the subsequent scare. Surfers are more aware of their surroundings and for the most part are using better judgement, not paddling out near the mouths of rivers, where run-off carries dead animals and other debris that sharks feed on, and by not paddling out alone at dusk and dawn, particularly in murky waters, where tiger shark prefer to hunt.

A surfer suffered serious leg wounds after being attacked by a tiger shark last October off Kauai while surfing in murky water near the mouth of the Wallua River . . .

Surfers, meanwhile, still are watching the horizon for more than the next set of waves, but are more comfortable knowing there are fewer sharks or "the guys in the grey suits" as they call them.

Los Angeles Times, 9 March 1994

QUEENSLAND, AUSTRALIA, 1992

The father of shark attack victim Michael Docherty said last night he had warned his son to beware of killer sharks at Moreton Island. "My last words to him on Tuesday were to take care, to be careful of sharks," Mr. Bill Docherty said last night as he battled to cope with the loss of his only son.

A massive white pointer [great white] shark savaged Docherty for twenty minutes before being forced to release the dead body in a horrifying attack off Moreton Island yesterday. Docherty, 28, of Palm Beach on the Gold Coast, died when the 4.2-metre shark rammed him and then towed him under water with his board—attached by a leg rope—often still visible above the waves.

His father said: "He was very much aware of the dangers. He told me he saw a bronze whaler shark down at Duranbah just last week." Mr. Docherty and his wife Dell said that their son had fallen in love with surfing and fishing as a four-year-old boy. "He was very keen on sport, very outgoing and very healthy. He never smoked and hardly drank, if at all. He loved the outdoors."

Up to fifteen other surfers, including two of Docherty's close friends, watched helplessly from the North Point beach. The shark did not release its grip until Redcliffe police officer Sergeant Phil Sharpe and a holidaying school teacher rushed to the scene in a fishing boat. The two men shouted and revved the boat's engine to frighten the shark away.

Sergeant Sharpe said Docherty's two friends had raised the alarm at about 2:30 pm, when they ran 150 metres to the tiny North Point settlement for help. When the boat caught up with the shark, the surfboard, with leg rope intact, was still being towed upright through the water.

Docherty had arrived only yesterday morning to begin the holiday with his friends. They had surfed at the same spot for more than ten years. Sergeant Sharpe said the water was clear and he was confident the shark was a white pointer. "It was bigger than the boat. He played with the body for about twenty minutes. I'd say the surfer would have drowned."

Docherty, who remained under water for much of the attack, had been paddling only about thirty metres from shore when knocked off his board. He had been wearing a black wetsuit. A dent was left in the board from the impact of the initial attack.

Twenty-one people have been killed by sharks and another four are presumed to have been taken since records have been kept in Queensland.

Palm Beach surfer Brett Provost, 25, likened the attacking shark to a fisherman "playing with a line." He said he took photographs from the beach as the board was towed through the surf.

Gold Coast surfer John Snip, 18, said he saw at least forty-five centimetres of the shark's dorsal fin above the water. Several times the board was towed backwards and under the water. He said there had been talk of a big white pointer off the point. "I've surfed here for seven or eight years and you see the sharks playing around, but, up until now, they have not been aggressive." He said the sharks seemed to be attracted to the area by the dumping of rubbish from trawlers which constantly lined the beach.

Brisbane Courier-Mail, 2 October 1992

CALIFORNIA, USA, 1991

Two days after a great white shark bit him, a thirty-two-year-old surfer sat in a wheelchair and calmly described how he fought off the giant fish and swam to safety off the coast of Santa Cruz County.

"I vaguely recall trying to pry his jaws loose," a relaxed Eric Larsen said at Dominican Santa Cruz Hospital. "I hit him as hard as I could. The next thing I could feel was being pulled by the leash on my board. I got on my board and started to paddle for shore. I could sort of see a blood trail and I thought uh-oh, this isn't so good. I could see the blood spurting out on the left, so I clamped it."

Larsen was attacked on Monday morning while surfing with his brother Nick about eight and a half miles south of the Ano Nuevo State Reserve in Santa Cruz County.

After fighting off the shark, Larsen remembered first aid techniques he had learned while working on a ski patrol in Montana: he applied pressure to the artery on his arm to slow the bleeding. He had the strength to struggle to shore because he had been training for canoe races and had been paddling outrigger canoes every day this summer. As he approached the shore, a wave carried him on to the beach. He crawled out of the water and started yelling. The whole ordeal lasted about half an hour.

"It was so fast that I didn't get scared until I hit the beach," he said, with both arms and left leg bandaged. "It didn't feel all that painful."

Ben Burdette, a sixteen-year-old surfer, heard Larsen's cries, found him on the beach and phoned a bakery where he works to tell his boss to call for help.

Burdette's mother, Michelle Tummino, dashed to the beach. "Larsen told me where the main artery was and where to hold it," she said. "He told us his leg was getting cold and he told us to hold his foot up. We were joking and laughing to keep him conscious. I was afraid he would go under and I wouldn't know what to do."

The Davenport Fire and Rescue Squad administered first aid, and Santa Cruz paramedics packed him in pressurized pants to staunch the bleeding. He was flown by an Army helicopter to Dominican Hospital, where surgeons treated tears and gashes in his left leg and both arms. Fred Tomlinson, a plastic surgeon who treated Larsen, said Larsen received about 400 stitches and staples to close up what he called the worst shark bite injuries he had ever seen. Larsen was in surgery for ten hours.

Larsen should recover fully, Tomlinson said. His right forearm received the most severe injury when the muscles and tendons were severed by the bite. Tomlinson said Larsen will probably need up to six months of recuperation and physical therapy before he regains the full use of his right hand. Larsen is expected to be released from the hospital tomorrow and could be surfing again in six weeks, Tomlinson said.

"I hope to go back in," said Larsen with a smile. "The statistical probability of a second attack is pretty minimal."

San Francisco Chronicle, 4 July 1991

CALIFORNIA, USA, 1991

With bandages hiding deep tooth marks, a lucky surfer yesterday talked about the horror of staring into the eye of the great white shark that had him captured in its jaws.

"It was only a split second, but it was very terrifying," said John Ferreira, a thirty-two-year-old machinist who was recuperating yesterday at Stanford Medical Center. Looking tense and grim, with his elbow swathed in bandages, Ferreira still mustered a few jokes as he told the story of the vicious encounter which could have cost him his life.

The attack occurred about 8:15 am on Saturday as Ferreira was surfing 150 yards off the shore of Scott Creek, near Davenport, in Santa Cruz County. "I had just paddled into the line up, the take-off point on the waves," he said. "I was just about there and all of a sudden it felt like someone had dropped a Volkswagen on my back. The first thing I saw six or eight feet under water was its eyeball on the side of its face shaking in the furious manner they do."

Ferreira, of La Selva beach, Santa Cruz County, swam back to shore, where friends applied a tourniquet to his arm and stopped the bleeding by applying pressure to his back. He was flown by air ambulance to Stanford Medical Center.

The shark had apparently taken Ferreira and his surfboard in its mouth, the upper jaw closing down on Ferreira's arm and back, and the lower jaw closing upon his surfboard. "The surfboard saved my life," he said.

If it had not been for the surfboard, doctors believe that Ferreira would have lost his left arm and possibly suffered puncture wounds in his chest. Ferreira emerged from the incident with relatively slight injuries, suffering cuts and deep puncture wounds shaped like a crescent on his back. His wounds took an hour of surgery and about 100 stitches to close—far less time than the ten hours of surgery needed to repair the damage to another surfer, Eric Larsen, who was attacked in July also near Davenport. Unlike Larsen, who considered the attack a positive experience, Ferreira called it "the most negative experience of my life."

The attack appears typical of what some shark experts call the great white shark's "bite and spit" feeding strategy. John E. McCosker, director of San Francisco's Steinhart Aquarium, in *Pacific Discovery* magazine recently reviewed great white shark attacks and concluded that the huge fish usually inflict single, large wounds on prey such as seals and sea lions.

Ferreira does not blame the shark for mistaking him for a tasty seal because of his wet suit, but he said he is not ready to forgive the estimated fourteen- to eighteen-foot animal. "Last night I started thinking about it, and I woke up with a cold sweat and a tear in my eye," he said. "I could take a gun to his head and shoot him. It's an eye for an eye in this world."

San Francisco Chronicle, 9 October 1991

TASMANIA, AUSTRALIA, 1989

A young Tasmanian surfer survived an attack by a big shark yesterday by jumping off his board seconds before it struck. But quick-thinking Steven Jillett, 17, had to survive almost ten terror-filled minutes in the surf while the 2.7-metre shark first circled him then followed him to the beach after he had struggled back on to his board.

The attack occurred about eighty metres off the popular surfing beach at Shelly Point, about two kilometres north of Scamander on the east coast at about 2:20 pm. The shark's teeth-marks on Steven's borrowed surfboard show how close he came to serious injury or death.

Last night, Steven, a boarder at Launceston's Scotch-Oakburn College, relived the minutes that turned a carefree afternoon in the surf with his mates into a fight for survival. Later he telephoned his shocked parents, who recently moved from Zeehan, where his father was a Renison Ltd. metallurgist, to Geraldton in Western Australia.

Steven said he feared he would lose a leg or arm when he was floating almost helplessly in the water after the shark first struck.

He had started surfing at about 2:12 pm with seventeen-year-old twins Sean and Julian Larby, of nearby Beaumaris, with whose family he was staying. About six surfers were in the water when the shark appeared. Steven said he was lying on his surfboard preparing to catch a wave when he saw a dark shape move past him about one metre to his right and about thirty centimetres below the surface. He first thought it was a dolphin.

The shark circled in front of him, then moved to his left and behind him. It then moved about ten metres to his right before attacking.

"Its fin was up and it was a fair way out of the water," Steven said. "When it was about five metres away I jumped off the board and swam away. It sort of jumped out of the water, latched on to the board, thrashed it around a lot and then it must have turned it around a bit. Then it let go and I was yelling, 'Shark, shark,' at this time. The rest of the guys said, 'Quick get on your board, get on it, it's the safest place to be.'

"I had just been attacked so I wasn't too keen on that idea, but eventually I did. But, while I was in the water, it was just swimming around in between the board and me, just doing circles, and I was keeping as still as possible."

Hobart Mercury, 23 October 1989

NATAL, SOUTH AFRICA, 1989

A young Isipingo lifesaver was savaged by a shark while surfing at Isipingo Beach not far from the river mouth yesterday—the second victim of a shark attack there in nine months. And, by an amazing coincidence, the previous young shark victim was on the beach and ran for medical help.

The installation of shark nets at Isipingo has been a sore point for several years. Local lifesavers have made numerous pleas to the Isipingo Town Board, without success.

Mr. Sudesh Hansraj, 19, a member of the Isipingo Lifesaving Club, was body-surfing about 100 metres from the Isipingo River mouth with two other club members when he was attacked just before 6 pm. The trainee quantity surveyor was bitten twice on the left leg, once on the thigh and just below the knee.

Last night Mr. Hansraj of Delta Road, Isipingo Beach, underwent emergency surgery at the R. H. Khan Hospital. A spokesman for the hospital described his condition as "stable."

An eyewitness, who did not want to be named, said Mr. Hansraj and other members of the lifesaving club were about to start training for the forthcoming South African Surf Lifesaving Championships when the attack took place.

It was just before 6 pm when the shark attacked Mr. Hansraj. Fortunately for him, two others, Mr. Bahoo Jadwat and the club's vice captain, Mr. Sherwin Stanley, were with him and brought him out of the water quickly.

"The last shark victim, Sastri Naidoo, was a seventeen-year-old schoolboy at the time. He ran to a doctor's home for help."

Two doctors soon arrived and Mr. Hansraj was put on a drip before being taken to hospital.

Mr. Graeme Charter, deputy director of the Natal Sharks Board, said it was too early to say what type of shark was involved. "The victim is very lucky. He has two deep wounds—one thirty centimetres in length and the other about twelve centimetres. We have taken photographs of the wounds and by Monday we should be able to say what species of shark attacked him."

Durban Daily News, 21 January 1989

Shark victim Sudesh Hansraj, speaking from his hospital bed in Chatsworth, where he is recovering after being attacked by a shark at Isipingo beach last Friday, said the incident would not stop him from going back into the sea: "It could have happened to anyone . . ."

Sudesh said he and other colleagues were waiting to catch a wave when he was attacked.

"The water was quite clear and I did not see it. I just felt a terrific blow on my left leg and, as I turned around, I saw the shark with its mouth wide open. I screamed for help and luckily for me my colleagues were near by and they brought me to shore. Had it not been for them, I might have been dead . . ."

Durban Daily News, 23 January 1989

CAPE PROVINCE, SOUTH AFRICA, 1989

A twenty-one-year-old surfer has described from his hospital bed how he survived a nightmare attack by a shark at Mossel Bay's popular surf spot, The Point.

Still badly shocked by his close shave with the jaws of death, Niko von Broembsen of Somerset West is in a serious but stable condition in the intensive care unit of the George Hospital after several hours of emergency surgery. The shark's teeth tore away muscle from Niko's left calf, left upper leg and thigh, and left forearm. The force of the bite exposed bone and broke his forearm.

He was attacked at about 10:45 am yesterday by what is believed to be a great white shark while he and a friend, twenty-two-year-old Adam Harding of Gordon's Bay were surfing the inside break at The Point.

"I did not see a thing before the attack. Suddenly I was clamped to my board and I could not move," he said. "But I was conscious the whole time. I felt no pain until I reached the hospital. I can remember clearly how it started pulling me under water. I suppose it wanted to take me down so it could eat me, and it let go once and bit again in the same area.

"I saw the shark's eyes and twisted my right arm around, pushing my fingers into an eye. I just kept pushing my fingers in and it let go of me eventually.

"I was close to the rocks at the beach and I moved towards them. There Adam and another man picked me up and carried me to the beach. I knew about everything that was going on around me—I kept on yelling at them to tie tourniquets around my arm and leg to stop the bleeding because I was bleeding badly."

Niko said that, as he was drifting to the rocks, the shark followed and he could see the big dorsal fin in the water behind him. "I was lucky, man. I could have been dead. Adam is my best buddy—if it wasn't for him, I would have been dead now."

Asked if he would surf again, he said: "No way. Well, I don't know. Yes, I'll probably go back into the water. That is, if I can ever walk properly again."

Meanwhile, there might soon be a price on the head of the shark. Mossel Bay Mayor Mr. Johan Oosthuizen, said he would suggest his council should offer a reward for the fisherman who landed the huge great white thought to be responsible for this attack and others on ski-boats. However, he added: "I do not believe we should overreact because of the attack. In the past sixty years there have been only three attacks in the area from Little Brak River to Hartenbos, and this one was the first in twenty to twenty-five years."

None the less the town is abuzz at this latest incident and local fishermen, already on the warpath against the shark because of recent attacks on ski-boats, have surrounded the area with baited buoys and line in the hope of catching the culprit.

Durban Daily News, 23 August 1989

NEW SOUTH WALES, AUSTRALIA, 1989

Adam McGuire can thank a school of dolphins for saving him from a shark which attacked him yesterday while he was surfing on the New South Wales north coast.

A local ambulance spokesman said that a group of dolphins chased off a shark which attacked Adam, 17, at Half Tide Beach, near Ballina, leaving him with a severely lacerated abdomen, at about 5:15 pm. Two companions managed to get him ashore and raise the alarm. Ambulance officers and a rescue helicopter were summoned to the beach. He was rushed to Lismore Base Hospital, where he was in a "satisfactory" condition last night.

Adam was on the second day of a holiday in the area with two companions, Brad Thompson and Jason Maloney, all from Newcastle. The three were riding 1.5-metre waves among a school of about fifteen or twenty dolphins. According to Brad Thompson, they noticed the dolphins start to get restless.

"All of a sudden, they started speeding up and swimming under us and we thought they were up to something," he said. "I looked over and saw Adam knocked off his board. I could see a hole in his board, and Adam in the water close to it. I saw the shark come up to him. He started hitting it in the head, trying to get it away from him. Then we didn't see it any more and we took Adam in to shore."

Police have asked Mr. John Hajje, operations manager at Manly Underwater World, to identify the shark from a plaster cast of the bite on the surfboard.

"I can't be sure until I see the bite, but, from the description they gave me, it appears to have been quite a big one, about four metres, and in that area it's probably a tiger," Mr. Hajje said. The bite was about thirty centimetres across with individual tooth marks measuring 6 cm × 4 cm.

He said Adam could probably thank his surfboard as much as the dolphins for his survival. "The police told me that, when the shark attacked, it took a chunk out of the board and he fell off," he said. "Rather than attack him, it kept on going for the board. It really just brushed him and didn't take much of a bite."

Sydney Morning Herald, 4 January 1989

ACAPULCO, MEXICO, 1980s

In the late 1980s, while avid American windsurfer Mike Schecter was surfing with his buddies in Acapulco, a decidedly irate shark, swimming at an alarming speed, made its way towards the group.

Everyone quickly paddled for the beach, but the shark popped up right beneath one fellow's board, chomping and snapping. Following a dramatic struggle, the surfer managed to catch a wave into the beach, followed by the shark, which unsuccessfully chased him on to the sand.

Frustrated, the shark turned away and headed down the coast, leaving the surfers with a premonition of bad things to come. Sure enough, a Canadian tourist was reportedly eaten later that day.

Windsurfing, September–October 1993

CAPE PROVINCE, SOUTH AFRICA, 1987

The sea "boiled with streaks of blood" when a massive shark savaged a Fish Hoek man surfing at Groot Jongersfontein, near Stilbaai, yesterday afternoon, an eyewitness told this paper.

Diver Mr. Fanie Oosthuizen, who saw the attack on surfer Mr. Peter John McCallum, 24, of Carmichael Road, said the surfer's board had saved him from an "almost certain death": "He was lying on his surfboard, which prevented the shark from biting him in half."

The attack occurred about 100 metres from the shore near a sandbank in water with a depth of a half to one and a half metres.

Mr. McCallum's mother, Mrs. Mary McCallum, said from Riversdale last night that her son was "fine" in Riversdale Hospital and was "resting quietly" after a two-hour operation, during which he received about 125 stitches. "We are extraordinarily fortunate: the shark's teeth must have slipped off the board." The shark had ripped "a large half-moon shaped" chunk out of the surfboard.

Her son sustained deep gashes to his right side, where the shark's jaws had gouged out pieces of flesh as it slipped on the board, Mrs. McCallum said.

Mr. Oosthuizen, a Groot Jongersfontein farmer, said he was diving at about 11:30 am, when he heard "a piercing scream further out in the breakers."

"I heard him scream, 'Bite,' and thought he was warning me that a dog was attacking my little daughter on the beach. But, when I looked back again, I heard him scream, 'I've been bitten, I've been bitten.' Then I saw this huge tail about a metre long and realized he was being attacked by a shark."

Mr. Oosthuizen then swam to one side to get a clearer view and saw a shark about three metres long—"then the water just boiled with blood."

"I swam up to him and he said, 'I don't want to die, I don't want to die.' Then he became calm and I said to him, 'Rascals don't die.' "

The two then swam to shore.

At the time of the attack Mr. McCallum's girl-friend, Miss Jo-Anne Bosman, of Bergvliet, and another woman surfer were further out to sea. Another surfer went to help the two women and the three reached shore safely.

Mr. Oosthuizen described Mr. McCallum as "a big man about 1.95 metres tall with broad shoulders" and said the shark's teeth marks extended from his spine, around under his arm, along his side with a few gashes on his thigh. Some of the shark's teeth, which were longer than a centimetre, were stuck in the surfboard, Mr. Oosthuizen added.

"He spoke to me when we got to shore and, despite his ribs showing from the shark bite and deep gashes on his side, he remained calm. He told me: 'I was lying on my board paddling out to catch a wave, when I noticed a large shark near me. I just lay still because they usually go away if you don't move. The next moment it went into a frenzy and attacked me.' "

Cape Times, 14 September 1987

CAPE PROVINCE, SÓUTH AFRICA, 1985

A boogie-boarder's leg was gashed today when he was attacked by a shark while swimming at East London. The shark has been identified as a great white from a tooth extracted from the surfer's wound.

The attack happened at 8 am, when Mr. Patrick Gee, 24, was swimming with a boogie-board on Eastern Beach. Mr. Gee apparently saw the shark come at him and tried to fend it off with the board.

The shark evaded the board and bit Mr. Gee on the right leg below the knee. He managed to reach the beach and was taken to the Frere Hospital by a motorist. He is reported to be in no danger.

The beach manager, Mr. L. O. Branfield, immediately banned bathing on the beach.

Durban Daily News, 24 October 1985

SOUTH CAROLINA, USA, 1985

A Tifton girl was riding the last wave of the day with her father and a friend at Folly Beach, South Carolina, when a shark suddenly attacked and seriously injured the youngster.

Julie Steed, 10, who was bitten on the left leg last Friday by what is believed to have been an eight- to nine-foot-long tiger shark, is being transferred to Emory University hospital from a hospital in Charleston. She could be admitted to Emory as early as next Tuesday, said Deborah Steed, the girl's mother. But Mrs. Steed is still chilled by the irony that Julie, her father, David Steed, and friend Brittany Walker of Tifton had decided to call it a day just moments before the attack.

"They were actually coming in when she was bitten," said Julie's mother. "They had a two-man raft, and just wanted to ride that last little surf in."

Julie, who was admitted to Roper Hospital in Charleston, lost two-thirds of her calf muscle as a result of the attack, but doctors are confident that she will be able to walk, Mrs. Steed said. The youngster, who had "too many stitches to count," will have to undergo extensive reconstructive and cosmetic surgery, her mother added.

Julie said she did not see the shark which bit her as she, her father and Brittany played in the surf only twenty feet from shore. "It was a total surprise, but I tried not to panic. I tried to stay calm," said Julie, who will be a fifth-grader in the fall. "The water was just a little bit above my knees, and, when a wave would come, to the bottom of my bathing suit."

John Jones, a spokesman for the Florida-based Cooperative Shark Attack Data Center [now the International Shark Attack File], said Julie most likely was attacked by a tiger shark eight or nine feet long, judging from the shark's biting pattern. The bite was about fourteen inches long, he said. Jones, who has been working with Folly Beach police and the Steed family to gather information about the attack, said Steed helped save his daughter's life by holding on to her when the shark struck.

"The shark apparently felt the resistance and let go. But he still dealt more damage than any attack I've dealt with up here," said Jones.

Sharks regularly go to shallow water to feed, but any number of things could have caused this particular shark to attack. "There are a lot of sandbars in the area. He could've gotten in and then felt trapped," said Jones.

Meanwhile, the eight-man police force in Folly Beach has been plagued with reports of shark sightings and swimmers being bumped, said Folly Beach

215

Police Chief George Tittle. So far, no sharks have been found, he said.

Atlanta Constitution, 23 July 1985

NATAL, SOUTH AFRICA, 1985

The hero of yesterday's shark attack on the south coast today described his horror when a shark two metres long "climbed on to the back" of his surfing friend.

The victim was top Natal surfer Bruce Eldridge, 18, who was savaged off an unprotected beach at Umbogintwini while surfing in conditions which the Natal Anti Shark Measure Board warned today are ideal for shark attack.

Doctors were today optimistic that they had saved Bruce's foot. Bruce, who lives at Athlone Park, had a large portion of his right calf and foot bitten off. He was rushed to Kingsway Clinic and then to Durban's Addington Hospital, where he had a long operation to repair damaged tissue. He left the theatre at 3 am.

"It sounds hopeful that the foot will be saved," Dr. Ralph McCarter, deputy medical superintendent at Addington Hospital, said today. But it was still too early to be sure. His condition was satisfactory, added Dr. McCarter.

Bruce was surfing near murky water at the mouth of the Umbogintwini River with his friends, Eric Robinson, 24, a Technikon student, and Mr. Keith Lowes, late yesterday when the incident occurred.

Mr. Robinson said a large chunk of the calf of Bruce's right leg was bitten out by the shark. His foot was also badly lacerated. He said the attack took place at about 6:30 pm.

"We were paddling out for a wave, when Bruce started shouting. I turned to see what was happening and I saw him being pulled from the board into an upright position. Then he was down on the board and it looked as if the shark—it must have been more than two metres long—was climbing on to his back.

"The water suddenly went red with blood. I got a huge fright. I started paddling towards him—I didn't think about it at all. A wave came and, when it had passed, I saw that the shark had gone.

"Bruce and I paddled to the shore. I used a towel to make a tourniquet. Keith and I then carried Bruce to the car. He was very white, but I think he was still conscious. I don't think he saw his leg. He didn't look at it. I think his mind was wandering a bit. He was saying odd things: one time he asked if he was allowed to cry."

Mr. Lowes said Bruce had not bled much as they rushed him to Kingsway Clinic and then to Addington Hospital: "He was very quiet. I kept asking him if he was still awake. I think he must have been in shock."

Mr. Robinson said they had been surfing at the beach for about ten years and there had never been a shark attack there: "It had a reputation for being a safe beach even though it was unprotected. I'm certainly not going to do it again."

Bruce, a second-year student at the University of Natal in Durban, won the Southern Natal Surfing

trials at Greenpoint at the weekend and took part in the recent South African Surfing Championships.
Durban Daily News, 18 January 1985

TRANSKEI, SOUTH AFRICA, 1982

Five surfers watched in horror as a Port Elizabeth student was dragged from his surfboard and under the water by a shark on the Transkei Wild Coast early yesterday morning.

Mr. Alex Macun, 27, chairman of the Port Elizabeth Technikon Students Representative Council and well-known freelance surfing photo-journalist, was attacked and killed just after 9:30 am at a secluded surfing spot, Ntlonyena, about thirty kilometres north of the Haven holiday resort.

Yesterday's attack is the second at Ntlonyena—notorious for its sharks—in just over a year. A Durban journalist, Mr. Simon Hammerton, 24, lost a leg in an attack in May last year.

Mr. Macun was a senior student at the Technikon's School of Art. His family lives in Cape Town and he is a SACS old boy.

A shocked witness to the attack, Mr. John Luyt, of Port Elizabeth, telephoned his father, Mr. Peter Luyt of Walmer, thirty minutes after the attack. "He was in a severe state of shock and told me he was surfing near by when a huge shark grabbed Alex . . . and the shark just disappeared under the water with Alex in his jaws. It appeared as if there was nothing they could do. John was in such a state of

218

shock that he called me first before informing the police," Mr. Luyt said.

A Transkei police spokesman said: "From what we understand, the man did not appear again. His friends scattered and paddled for the safety of the beach. The surfers then raced to a trading store at Hobeni, where they informed the authorities and relatives."

Mr. Harland Woods, who owns the trading store, said that the men were severely shocked. "My store is about ten kilometres from the beach where Mr. Macun and his friends were surfing."

Police have been unable to recover Mr. Macun's body, which was spotted in the small bay late yesterday afternoon.

Mr. Macun's death happened on the eve of the start of South Africa's premier surfing event, the Gunston 500. The editor of a surfing magazine, Mr. Paul Naude, said that Mr. Macun was one of the best contributors to his publication.

The director of the Technikon, Professor P. D. Veldsman, said he was shocked by his SRC chairman's death. "He was an outstanding personality and a great thinker. Alex was an inspiration to everyone with whom he came in contact."

Mr. Macun leaves his recently widowed mother, Mrs. Bertha Macun, two brothers and a sister.

Mr. Simon Hammerton, who was attacked at the same spot just over a year ago, said from his Durban home last night that he was terribly shocked to hear of the attack. He said the Wild Coast had become a notorious place for shark attacks and that it was not wise for people to surf at the same place where someone else had been attacked. "How many more

people have to be attacked before they realize this?"
Cape Times, 30 June 1982

CALIFORNIA, USA, 1981

The shark-torn body of missing surfer Lewis Boren was pulled out of the surf near Pacific Grove on Thursday, ending the torment of uncertainty for his family in Torrance.

Monterey County Coroner Harvey Hillbun said the experienced twenty-four-year-old kneeboard surfer, a graduate of Torrance High School, was the victim of "a classic example of a shark bite."

Boren had been missing since last Saturday, and his surfboard found on Sunday, bearing teeth fragments and blood stains around an eighteen-inch gash. Hillbun said Boren was probably lying on the board waiting for a good wave just outside the breakers when the shark, believed to be a great white shark more than eighteen feet long and weighing at least two tons, moved in, "his mouth open, lunging toward his prey."

"When the shark bit, he had both the board and Lewis in his mouth," Hillbun said. "There's a large portion of his upper torso gone, from beneath the left armpit to just above the hip."

The body, clad in a dark wetsuit, was recovered from the surf by a park ranger. It was tentatively identified by a tattoo on the shoulder. Searchers had been scouring beaches and the coastal waters for a sign of Boren since discovering his chewed-up kneeboard, which is smaller than a regular surfboard and is ridden in the kneeling position.

Before the body was located, analysis had begun on blood samples found on the board, and officials of the Steinhart Aquarium in San Francisco started comparing the tooth marks with their extensive collection of shark jaws in hopes of discovering Boren's fate.

The victim's mother, Ella Boren, said Lewis began surfing in junior high school and was an accomplished surfer and water skier. He also enjoyed snow skiing, she said.

"Lewis was supposed to come down yesterday—we talked to him last Friday," Mrs. Boren said as the family began gathering for a sad Christmas. "We had his presents all wrapped."

Before Monterey authorities called with news of the body, Mrs. Boren said the family still held out hope. "It would be a miracle if he shows up, we know that. But not knowing, you can't help but hope."

Boren lived in a camper truck outside the Monterey engineering firm where he worked as a welder. He once attended El Camino Community College in Carson.

Experts have calculated that the shark was the largest known to prowl off the California coast and may have reached twenty-one feet. The largest great white ever captured measured twenty-one feet and was nabbed off Cuba. Sharks up to forty feet have been reported, but never captured. Surfers have been wary of the Monterey Bay waters since Boren vanished and a marine scientist said on Thursday that a rash of reported shark sightings was actually a school of about eighty large grey and white dolphins which entered the bay.

Los Angeles Times, 25 December 1981

NATAL, SOUTH AFRICA, 1975

A shark yesterday savaged a sixteen-year-old surfer, Bretton Jones, at Amanzimtoti, completely severing his right foot.

Bretton and two friends, Steven van der Welde, 15, and Justin Philip, 17, were surfing in an area unprotected by shark nets at the time of the attack. Bretton is the sixth person to be attacked at Amanzimtoti [see chapter 1] since January 1974.

"I never saw the shark, I just felt something grab me on the leg and try to pull me off my board. When I resisted, it shook me like a dog," Bretton told helpers on the beach.

He underwent an emergency operation at Addington Hospital yesterday afternoon. Doctors removed about another eight centimetres of his leg to clean the wound. He was in a satisfactory condition last night. "We can only thank God that he was not injured more seriously. It was an accident and could have been much worse," Bretton's mother, Mrs. D. J. Jones, said yesterday, shortly after returning from Addington Hospital. Bretton is a standard nine pupil at Kingsway High School. He is one of a family of four children.

"We were about fifty metres from the shore. Bretton and I were both sitting on our surfboards when he suddenly screamed, 'Shark, shark,' and started paddling back to the beach," said Steven van der Welde. "I looked up and saw a fin and knew that it had attacked Bretton by the amount of blood."

Yesterday's attack on Bretton carried the grim co-incidence that it marked—almost to the day—the first anniversary of the attack that cost his schoolmate, Damon Kendrick, a leg last year [see page 160].

Cape Times, 24 February 1975

NEW SOUTH WALES, AUSTRALIA, 1951

The horribly mauled body of Frank Okulich, 21, Australian surf ski champion, was washed into shallow water at Merewether Beach, Newcastle, at 4 pm today, an hour after a shark had dragged him under.

The shark took Okulich 100 yards from the shore, just after three other lifesavers swimming with him had caught a wave into the beach. Only a dark shadow, about eight feet long, was seen in the water when he was dragged under. His body disappeared.

The man who saw the attack from the beach, but who would not give his name, said: "There were four chaps swimming about 100 yards out at the southern end of the beach. Three chaps took a shoot in, but Okulich missed it. Then I saw a shadow in the crest of a big wave. It tugged the poor kid under, but he came up again waving his arms.

"I saw the shadow, which was bigger than a man, attack him again and again. Then his head just bobbed in the waves like a cork. After about four minutes I saw the shark have another go at him. Then his body disappeared. The sun was shining on the waves and you could almost see right through each breaker as it built up."

Okulich had been swimming with Merewether lifesavers Bill Morgan, 24, of Ranclaude Street, John Blackett, 30, of Ridge Street, and James Robert Johns, 25, of Janet Street. Morgan and another Merewether lifesaver, Ron Galbraith, went out on surf skis immediately they heard Okulich was being attacked. They could not find his body.

Merewether beach inspector K. Ayton said: "I saw a big pool of blood on the water just after it happened."

Inspectors closed the beach. Two hundred girls from a Newcastle high school had left the water a few minutes before the tragedy.

Lifesavers at Newcastle Beach manned a surf boat and surf skis and rowed to Merewether, about two miles away. They began a search for Okulich's body. A large crowd lined the promenade. At 4 pm a youth pointed to shallow water. A lifesaver, Robert Mather, of Frederick Street, Merewether, dashed into the surf and recovered Okulich's mutilated body. The shark had mauled him on every part except his head.

Several women in the crowd wept when they saw his body carried out of the water.

Okulich belonged to the Dixon Park Lifesaving Club and lived with his widowed mother in Rose Street, Merewether. He had two sisters, Mrs. Ielene [sic] Peterson, of Lambton, Newcastle, and Miss Renie Okulich, a schoolteacher at Lakemba. Okulich won the Australian single surf ski championship at Perth on 24 March. He joined the Dixon Park club as a young boy learning to swim.

His parents came from Poland before he was born and his father died when he was a baby.

The last shark fatality at Newcastle was in January 1949, when a Newcastle lifesaver, Ray Land, 20, was killed.

Sydney Morning Herald, 7 December 1951

6
Stranger than Fiction

CALIFORNIA, USA, 1994

A shark ripped open a man's arm in a night club four miles from the ocean. Doctors needed 100 stitches to close the wound.

Steve Rosenbloome was bitten on Monday as he tried to move the four-foot lemon shark and another shark from the sixteen-foot tank they had outgrown at the Shark Club billiard hall. The animals were headed to the Scripps Institute of Oceanography at La Jolla.

"I got bit by a land shark," joked the thirty-three-year-old fish handler after arriving at the hospital emergency room.

Associated Press, 9 March 1994

AUSTRALIA, 1937

Having sailed home [to Falmouth, England] from Port Germain, Australia, by way of the Cape of Good Hope, the Finnish four-mast barque *Penang* took 139 days to complete the passage.

The captain relates that, while the vessel was at Port Germain, bathers on the beach were horrified at seeing a tiger shark rise out of the water with a man's body in its mouth.

The body was that of one of the crew of the *Penang*, who had been drowned on the previous night. Captain Karlson manned a boat and chased the shark, firing several pistol shots at it, but it was not seen again. The body was, however, recovered.

On the previous night some members of the crew had overloaded a small boat when returning from a dance to the ship. The craft capsized in a rough sea and a seaman and the ship's carpenter were drowned. The other ten occupants of the boat were saved.

Captain Karlson said that the vessel made a very good start and had an average passage of ninety-six days to the Cape of Good Hope. The *Penang* sailed through the Azores, but lay in the doldrums for some time and failed to get the advantage of the trade wind. When approaching the English Channel, she encountered a heavy fog, which compelled Captain Karlson to remain on the bridge for forty-eight hours.

The Times, London, 13 July 1937

IRELAND, 1937

A woman's shoe and what is thought to be a human bone were found in the maw of a thirty-foot shark that was caught after a great struggle at Keel Bay, Achill, Ireland, yesterday.

Hundreds of visitors watched the fight, which lasted for several hours, before the shark could be brought into shallow water and shot dead.

The Times, London, 5 August 1937

FLORIDA, USA, 1982

A fisherman on Saturday reeled in a 364-lb tiger shark stuffed with the complete leg of a man and a bone from another leg, authorities said.

Dr. Ronald Wright, a medical examiner for Broward County, said a man's right leg with a sock and a tennis shoe, and an upper left thigh bone were found in the nine-and-a-half-foot shark, which had put up a four-hour fight with the fisherman. Wright said the shark's jaw measured fifteen inches in diameter.

Steve Cory, an investigator with the medical examiner's office, said that, when the fishermen brought the shark ashore and opened its mouth, "The leg popped out—literally."

Wright speculated that the victim was dead before encountering the shark.

"Now we're working on looking for traces of drugs and alcohol in the victim. That's a very important part of the puzzle," Wright said, adding that it might take several days to turn up such evidence. "In South Florida waters we just don't have sharks attack swimmers. For the last twenty plus years, the only ones we've ever seen are individuals who have drowned, usually because of intoxication, or killed by other means and dumped in the water."

Based on the size of the recovered bones, the unidentified victim was believed to have been about six feet tall, in his twenties and weighed about 190 lbs. Wright said the man probably had been dead from one to four days, based on what is known about the normal digestion time for tiger sharks. He said he thinks the attack took place within 100 miles of the spot where the shark was caught. Experts have told him that tiger sharks rarely travel more than twenty-five miles a day, he said.

"I've been on the phone with medical examiners in Hawaii, where there are lots of shark attacks," he said. "They told me their usual experience is to find the shark relatively close to where the event happened, not more than even a few miles."

Hollywood [Florida] police detective Ron Hickman said the shark was caught at 5:30 am EDT about one and a quarter miles from Hollywood in the Atlantic Ocean. It was reeled in by Al Laurino, 36, a sport fisherman and custom fishing-rod manufacturer from Davie.

"I've been fishing for sharks for over fifteen years and I've caught a lot of sharks, cut them all open, and I've never run across anything like this," Laurino said. "Usually you just find a lot of fish inside them."

He agreed with Wright that the victim was dead before encountering the shark. "For one thing, there was a sneaker on the person, so you know he wasn't out diving. And another thing—tiger sharks mainly feed on the bottom. There's no doubt the body was laying on the bottom when the shark came along."

New Orleans Times-Picayune, 5 September 1982

SOUTH CAROLINA, USA, 1988

Diners at a Metairie restaurant which features a giant aquarium got a real taste of deep-sea adventure when a diver in the tank was attacked by a six-foot tiger shark.

Wiley Beevers was feeding fish on Friday night in the tank in front of about fifty diners at Sharky's Reef Restaurant, 3505 N. Hullen Avenue, when the 120-lb shark tore into his arm. Beevers left the aquarium under his own power and was taken to East Jefferson Hospital, where he received seventy-five stitches to close the shark wound, said Jack Dunn, one of the restaurant's owners. Beevers was released from the hospital later, officials said.

Dunn said that he and other divers routinely go into the 135,000-gallon aquarium to feed lettuce to the fish in the ninety-foot-long tank. The shark had never before bothered a diver feeding other fish, he said. "When he sees we have nothing but lettuce, he usually swims away."

Beevers, a Metairie lawyer, had been in the tank to feed the fish several times, Dunn said. Beevers could not be reached on Monday for comment.

The sharks are fed shad, mullet and other fish every three days by more experienced divers, Dunn said. He added that diners usually enjoy watching divers feed the fish, but they were alarmed when they saw the attack and Beevers' blood swirl to the surface.

"They got to see something a lot of people hope they'll never get to see," Dunn said. "They were concerned for the diver and were relieved to see he was OK."

New Orleans Times-Picayune, 23 August 1988

FLORIDA, USA, 1990

Two sneaker-clad human feet were found in the stomach of a shark caught off the north-east coast of Florida, at Mayport.

The Times, London, 25 May 1990

LONDON, UNITED KINGDOM, 1995

A mother and her three children were treated by ambulance men yesterday . . . after inhaling fumes from a dead shark. The one-foot fish, kept in formaldehyde and other toxic chemicals, had been left at their home in Brentford, London.

The People, London, 16 April 1995

Unprovoked Shark Attacks Reported Worldwide 1990–95

Information kindly supplied by the International Shark Attack File and based on attacks reported to them.

	YEAR	TOTAL ATTACKS	FATAL	NON-FATAL		YEAR	TOTAL ATTACKS	FATAL	NON-FATAL
WORLD	1990	34	2	32	HONG	1990	0	0	0
	1991	33	3	30	KONG	1991	1	1	0
	1992	47	5	42		1992	0	0	0
	1993	50	12	38		1993	2	2	0
	1994	57	7	50		1994	0	0	0
	1995	62	11	51		1995	3	3	0
Totals:		283	40	243					
					JAPAN	1990	0	0	0
AUS-	1990	2	0	2		1991	0	0	2
TRALIA	1991	4	1	3		1992	3	1	2
	1992	3	1	2		1993	1	0	1
	1993	3	2	1		1994	1	0	1
	1994	0	0	0		1995	1	1	0
	1995	1	1	0					

Alex MacCormick

	YEAR	TOTAL ATTACKS	FATAL	NON-FATAL		YEAR	TOTAL ATTACKS	FATAL	NON-FATAL
BRAZIL	1990	2	1	1	NEW	1990	2	0	2
	1991	0	0	0	ZEALAND	1991	0	0	0
	1992	6	0	6		1992	2	0	2
	1993	5	1	4		1993	1	0	1
	1994	14	2	12		1994	0	0	0
	1995	5	2	3		1995	1	0	1
REUNION	1990	1	0	1	FLORIDA	1990	9	0	9
ISLAND	1991	1	0	1		1991	12	0	12
	1992	3	2	1		1992	13	0	13
	1993	0	0	0		1993	7	0	7
	1994	1	1	0		1994	22	0	22
	1995	1	1	0		1995	29	0	29
SOUTH	1990	4	1	3	HAWAII	1990	1	0	1
AFRICA	1991	3	0	3		1991	4	1	3
	1992	3	0	3		1992	6	1	5
	1993	6	0	6		1993	4	0	4
	1994	9	1	8		1994	3	1	2
	1995	3	1	2		1995	1	0	1
USA									
CALI-FORNIA	1990	5	0	5	OTHER	1990	8	0	8
	1991	3	0	3	PARTS	1991	5	0	5
	1992	2	0	2	OF	1992	6	0	6
	1993	4	0	4	WORLD	1993	17	7	10
	1994	1	1	0		1994	6	1	5
	1995	4	0	4		1995	13	2	11

Chronological List of Attacks Included in this Book

13.9.37		steamer rammed, Clyde	UK	136
28.10.37	F	N. Girvan, surfer, Queensland	Aus	93
30.8.38	F	British sailor	HK/Chin	134
3.10.40	F	M. Farrin (13), swimmer, NSW	Aus	169
4.1.42	F	Z. Steadman (f), standing, Sydney	Aus	32
26.12.42	F	D. Burch (f,15), paddling, Sydney	Aus	34
30.7.45	F	USS *Indianapolis* sunk, near Guam	S. Pacific	122
23.10.51	F	swimmer, Northern Queensland	Aus	169
7.12.51	F	F. Okulich, surf champion, NSW	Aus	223
1.3.54	F	lifesaver, Sydney	Aus	31
10.7.54		E. Marks, Br swimmer	Bermuda	168
16.7.54	F	refugee swimmer, Trieste/Fiume	Italy	144
29.7.54	F	Br sailor, swimmer	Singapore	122
17.9.54	F	Br sailor, swimmer	HK	121
7.10.54		deckhand hurt, Isle of Man	UK	121
13.1.55	F	J. Willis (13), spearfishing, Sydney	Aus	31
6.2.55	F	B. Rautenberg, swimmer, Sydney	Aus	29
8.7.55	F	W. F. Dixon (f), swimmer, Red Sea	Yemen	167
56		girl (14), swimmer	VA/US	10
6.3.56	F	J. Wishart, lifesaver	Aus	166
27.6.56	F	fisherman	Madeira	121
21.7.56	F	J. Smedley, swimmer, Valletta	Malta	144
18.12.57		R. Wherley, Karridene	SA	28
20.12.57	F	A. Green (14), swimmer, Uvongo	SA	162
23.12.57	F	V. Berry, swimmer, Margate	SA	164
30.12.57	F	Julia Painting (14), swimmer, Margate	SA	21
9.1.58	F	D. Prinsloo, paddler, Scottburgh	SA	25
3.4.58	F	N. Badenhorst, bather, Port Edward	SA	27
5.4.58	F	Fay Bester, bather, Uvongo	SA	29
17.11.59	?	airline passengers, Gulf of Mexico	Mex/US	118
14.12.59	F	child boat passenger	Indian O.	118
30.12.61	F	Margaret Hobbs, swimmer, Sydney	Aus	19
10.12.62	F	G. Corner, diver, Normansville	Aus	91
28.1.63	F	Marcia Hathaway, paddler, Sydney	Aus	15
9.12.63		R. Fox, spearfisherman, Adelaide	Aus	58
29.11.64		H. Bource, diver, Lady Julia Percy Is.	Aus	88
28.2.66		swimmer (13) mauled, Coledale	Aus	162
14.6.66		Naples bathers threatened	Italy	15
21.8.66	F	L. Etwat (f, 9) + M. Bosket (f, 13)	N Guinea	161
26.9.66		B. Davidson, skindiver, Queensland	Aus	88
15.5.67		fisherman loses tooth	Gibraltar	117
21.8.67	F	R. Bartle, spearfisherman, Jurien Bay	Aus	86

Date		Description	Location	No.
1.12.69		G. Cartwright, up Swan River, Perth	Aus	13
24.9.70	F	14 boat passengers	W. Pacific	117
73		B. Curtsinger, Caroline Is, Micronesia	Pacific	85
73		boy, crabbing, False Bay	VA/US	11
7.1.74		L. Pyper, lifesaver, Amanzimtoti	SA	158
13.2.74		D. Kendrick + J. Kool, Amanzimtoti	SA	160
2.7	F	Horne family shipwrecked	Panama	96
17.8.74	F	Chinese escapee, swimmer	HK	157
23.2.75		B. Jones, surfer, Amanzimtoti	SA	222
26.75		Russian seaman	Indian O.	115
3.76		various attacks	UK	1
15.9.80	?	air crash victims	Bahamas	114
3.10.80		G. EuDaly + C. Castonguay, divers	FLA/US	83
15.6.81		fishing boat attacked, Isle of Wight	UK	113
10.8.81	F	C. Wapniarski, swimmer, Ormond Beach	FLA/US	156
25.8.81		T. Best, snorkeler, Gulf Island	FLA/US	82
20.9.81	F	M. Meeker, swimmer, Tampa Bay	FLA/US	155
18.10.81		R. Kiefling, surfer, Cocoa Beach	FLA/USA	11
21.10.81		V. H. Ely, swimmer, Jupiter Beach	FLA/US	11
25.12.81	F	L. Boren, surfer, Monterey	CA/US	220
20.3.82		attack on government vessel	FLA/US	112
30.6.82	F	A. Macun, surfer, Ntloyena, Transkei	SA	218
5.9.82	F	leg found in shark	FLA/US	229
26.9.82		M. Herder, diver, Mendocino Co.	CA/US	80
27.7.83	F	2 in ship capsize	Aus	110
17.8.83		J. Redenbaugh (f, 16), swimmer	VA/US	10
3.7.84		3 in fishing competition, Jacksonville	FLA/US	109
26.7.84		2 female swimmers	Tex/US	8
24.10.84		S. Fletcher (f), swimmer	FLA/US	7
5.1.85		D. James, diver, Cape Point	SA	79
18.1.85		B. Eldridge, surfer	SA	216
5.3.85	F	S. Durdin (f), diver, Port Lincoln	Aus	76
23.7.85		J. Steed (f, 10), on raft, Folly Beach	SC/US	214
24.10.85		P. Gee, surfer, East London	SA	213
7.12.86		F. Gallo, diver, Carmel	CA/US	74
23.12.86	F	W. R. Olls, swimmer	SA	154
20.4.87		A. Voglino (f), swimmer	Tex/US	5

14.9.87		P. McCallum, surfer, Stilbaai	SA	211
8.10.87	F	100 shipwreck victims, Dominica	Caribbean	107
24.8.88		diver in restaurant aquarium	SC/US	231
late '80s	F	anon swimmer	Mexico	211
4.1.89		3 surfers, NSW	Aus	209
21.1.89		S. Hansraj, surfer	SA	205
31.1.89	F	T. McCallister, R. Stoddard, kayakers	CA/US	104
4.2.89	F	L. Costanzo, diver, Tuscany	Italy	39
20.6.89		C. Loe, spearfisherman, Cocodrie	LA/US	72
23.8.89		N. Broembsen, surfer, Mossel Bay	SA	207
4.9.89		L. Stroup, diver, Channel Is	CA/US	70
18.9.89		G. van Niekerk, diver, False Bay	SA	69
23.10.89		S. Jillett, surfer, Tasmania	Aus	204
25.5.90	F	feet found in shark, Mayport	FLA/US	232
26.6.90	F	M. Price (f), skindiver, Mossel Bay	SA	68
9.9.90		R. Orr, abalone diver, Jenner	CA/US	64
16.9.90		L. French, diver, Farallon Is.	CA/US	65
8.6.91	F	T. Yeung (f), swimmer, Kowloon	HK	153
29.6.91	F	Chinese fisherman, Kowloon	HK	103
4.7.91		E. Larsen, surfer, Ano Nuevo	CA/US	200
2.8.91		waterbed, Sta Margherita Ligure	Italy	5
3.8.91		woman canoeist, Portofino	Italy	102
9.9.91	F	diver, Adelaide	Aus	61
9.10.91		J. Ferreira, surfer, Davenport	CA/US	202
3.12.91	F	M. Morrell (f), swimmer	Hawaii	152
2.10.92	F	M. Docherty, surfer, Moreton Island	Aus	197
24.10.92	F	K. Harada, diver, Gyogo Island	Japan	57
22.10.92		R. Gruzinsky, surfer, Oahu	Hawaii	195
13.1.93		canoeists crossing Atlantic	Caribbean	100
8.6.93	F	T. Cartwright (f), diver, Tasmania	Aus	42
10.6.93	F	J. Ford, scuba diver, Byron Bay	Aus	56
15.6.93	F	2 deaths in previous fortnight	HK	4
13.8.93		D. Miles, abalone diver	CA/US	55
9.93		S. Shoemaker, windsurfer, Hookipa	Hawaii	195
10.93		D. Schaumann (f), pregnant lifesaver	FLA/US	149
15.10.93		R. Johnson (f), kayaker	CA/US	98
25.11.93	F	3 UN workers, Mogadishu	E. Afric	3
9.3.94		attack in night club, Costa Mesa	CA/US	227
16.4.94	F	young woman, San Diego	CA/US	147
6.94	F	B. Corby, surfer, East London	SA	184
27.9.94		L. Kozarinova (f), swimmer, Hilton Head	SC/US	148

Shark Attacks

9.12.94	F	J. Robinson, diver, San Miguel Island	CA/US	51
10.1.95		M. Sullivan, surfer, Davenport	CA/US	190
1.6.95	F	Tso Kam-sun, diver, Sai Kung	HK	146
2.6.95	F	Herman Lo Cheuk-Yuet, swimmer	HK	145
15.6.95	F	woman swimmer	HK	2
30.6.95		M. Flagg, diver	CA/US	48
18.8.95		J. Oatley, Br surfer, Daytona	FLA/US	193
19.8.95	F	11 attacks 1994, Recife	Brazil	191
9.95		divers' near miss, Isle of Wight	UK	45
13.9.95	F	W. Covert, diver	FLA/US	46
1.12.95		K. Scollay, diver, Chatham Is.	NZ	43
14.1.96		4 fishermen sunk, NSW	Aus	95
9.3.96		J. Hotchkiss (f), Br. swimmer, Heron I.	Aus	141